Shine
from
Within

ANURAG PAUL

Embracing the Radiance of Enlightenment

Shine
from
Within

ANURAG PAUL

KALAMOS LITERARY SERVICES LLP

Kalamos Literary Services LLP

Email: info@kalamos.co.in | editorial@kalamos.co.in

Published in 2024 by

Kalamos Literary Services

ISBN- 978-81-19601-27-1

Copyright © *Anurag Paul* (2024)

Shine from Within : Embracing the Radiance of Enlightenment
Anurag Paul

Cover Designed & Typeset in Kalamos Literary Services LLP

Print and bound in India.

WHAT READERS ARE SAYING ABOUT *SHINE FROM WITHIN: EMBRACING THE RADIANCE OF ENLIGHTENMENT*

"If you're on a quest for self-discovery or simply curious about the intricate workings of relationships and the art of managing life gracefully, look no further. Anurag Paul's book, "Shine from Within: Embracing the Radiance of Enlightenment," is a literary gem that deserves a place on your reading list. This book is a captivating journey through a myriad of topics, seamlessly blending the realms of relationships, mental well-being, financial wisdom, and spirituality. It's like having a heart-to-heart conversation with a dear friend who shares their insights on life's most pressing questions. Anurag's writing is as versatile as it is relatable, making you feel like you're sitting across from him, engrossed in a compelling conversation. His words resonate with authenticity and wisdom, offering valuable guidance and a fresh perspective on the complexities of modern existence. Whether you're seeking profound insights or simply looking for an engaging read to broaden your horizons, "Shine from Within" has something for everyone. Prepare to be inspired, enlightened, and entertained as you embark on this enriching journey with Anurag Paul as your trusted guide."

Aditi Vyas, *Oxford University Alumni and Gender Specialist, New Delhi*

"This is a must-read and insightful book from Anurag Paul. This book will motivate you to unleash your potential to glint in yourself by putting great and vital ideas to enrich your life from within. Knowing Anurag Paul has been nothing short of amazing."

Worrell Daniel, *Life Transformation Coach, Ludhiana, Punjab*

"This book can be read in two ways. To begin, you read the book and believe that these words of wisdom came from a 'yogi' type of person who has lived for many years to ferment his life experiences to this level. Or you read about the author first and are astounded at how such a young person can brew such mature thoughts and relate to the lives of ordinary people. I have had both experiences. Anurag and I worked in the same team during the most terrible moment in human history - the COVID-19 period. He astounded me with his calm and collected demeanor mixed with great energy. This is the first of several books that will include his ideas and ideologies. Anurag offers practical suggestions and exercises to help readers apply the concepts to their own lives. The writing is straightforward, making it simple to understand and follow. Aside from the written book, I appreciate Anurag's soothing voice. His podcasts are as serene as his words and ideas. This book has something for everyone; for some, it has everything."

Ajai Kumar S, *Strategic Communications and Advocacy Expert, New Delhi*

"In our digital age, where virtual connections are just as significant as physical ones, the pursuit of meaningful and sustainable relationships has become paramount. How do we navigate this complex landscape to build relationships that not only endure but also nurture a productive and fulfilling life? "Shine From Within: Embracing the Radiance of Enlightenment" is the answer to the questions that may have been echoing in your mind about relationships, life's purpose, and the everyday dilemmas we all face. This book serves as a guiding light, a catalyst for personal growth, and a roadmap to discovering inner peace and contentment. Its wisdom will empower you to thrive in all aspects of life. Why do I speak of it with such confidence? Because I have had the privilege of knowing Anurag Paul since 2012, when he was my student in English Journalism course at the Indian Institute of Mass Communication (IIMC), North East Campus. Anurag stood out as a brilliant scholar, driven by a sincere and humble desire to learn and grow. Even as he achieved academic success, he faced his own share of physical, mental, and spiritual challenges. What I am most delighted to witness is how he has overcome these obstacles and transformed into the person of depth and wisdom that he is today. "Shine from Within: Embracing the Radiance of

Enlightenment" is born from Anurag's personal experiences, and his generosity in sharing these insights with others is both valuable and commendable. May this book enrich your life, and may you find the enlightenment and fulfillment that the author desires for all who embark on this enlightening journey."

Dr. C. Lalmuansangkimi, *Associate Professor, Centre for Media Studies, School of Social Sciences, Jawaharlal Nehru University, New Delhi*

"Anurag Paul, a seasoned journalist turned communication specialist, brings extensive expertise and a storytelling passion through his dynamic communication. With a strong educational background, Anurag's ability to forge partnerships and amplify grassroots voices underscores the transformative impact of effective dialogue. He continues to contribute meaningfully to the communication field through his podcast or his latest offering. "Shine From Within: Embracing the Radiance of Enlightenment" has the potential to become a valuable resource for those seeking personal growth, improved relationships, and holistic well-being."

Mohit Sharma, *Former journalist and conflict zone expert turned Crisis Communications Specialist, New Delhi*

"Within the pages of "Shine from Within: Embracing the Radiance of Enlightenment", I discovered a guide delicately weaving together the realms of mental health, relationships, and spiritual discovery. The book deeply resonates with the challenges and complexities of navigating a modern life and offers profound insights on how to develop meaningful relationships with the self and others. Through the book, Anurag creates an atmosphere of trust and compassion, inviting readers to embark on a journey of self-discovery and growth. Whether you are seeking to deepen your understanding of mental health, enhance your interpersonal relationships or simply gain a greater sense of empathy, "Shine from Within: Embracing the Radiance of Enlightenment" is an indispensable companion."

Priyanka Banerjee, *Gender Equity Strategist, New Delhi*

"In a world clamouring for guidance, introspection, and the secrets to a fulfilled life, "Shine from Within: Embracing the Radiance of Enlightenment" by Anurag Paul stands out as an illuminating beacon of wisdom and self-discovery. I'm excited to recommend this remarkable book that transcends the ordinary and dives deep into the realms of the human psyche and heart. Anurag Paul, a seasoned writer and sage observer of life's intricacies, has penned a work that goes beyond the surface of self-help literature. His words carry a profound psychological and emotional weight that resonates with readers, and this unique touch sets "Shine From Within: Embracing the radiance of Enlightenment" apart from the rest. The book's pages are adorned with the author's deep-rooted experiences and profound insights, making it a thought-provoking and timely masterpiece. In an era where many seek solace and meaning from within, Anurag's work offers much-needed guidance, solace, and encouragement. Anurag's expertise in the field shines through every line, weaving a tapestry of personal and interpersonal experiences. From the delicate art of self-care to the intricate nuances of relationships, mental health, and personal growth, the author leaves no stone unturned. "Shine From Within: Embracing the radiance of Enlightenment" is a roadmap to empowerment. It doesn't just offer advice; it nurtures self-belief, resilience, and a deeper understanding of life's dynamic journey. Anurag's words serve as both a guide and a companion, helping readers navigate the maze of existence with grace, confidence, and wisdom. I am convinced that this book will not only meet but exceed your expectations. If you're looking for a book that will empower you, awaken your inner potential, and shed light on the dynamics of your life's journey, then "Shine From Within: Embracing the radiance of Enlightenment" by Anurag Paul is your next must-read."

Banshanlang Marwein, *Assistant Professor, St. Anthony's College, Shillong, Meghalaya*

"In *Why You Should Never Lose Faith In God*, Anurag investigates deep into the human condition, through the lens of spirituality and faith; he masterfully navigates the elaborates balance between our desires and the wisdom to resist unchecked urges. In *Why John the Baptist is Important to the Christmas Story*, Anurag embarks on a profound exploration of the often-overlooked role of John the Baptist in the grand narrative of Christmas. Through careful examination of biblical passages, he illuminates the key position that John held in preparing the hearts of people for the arrival of Jesus Christ. Moreover, Anurag beautifully portrays John the Baptist as a chosen vessel of God, foretelling the Messiah's coming and fulfilling the prophecy written in Isaiah. He reminds us of the key moment when John baptized Jesus in the Jordan River, solidifying the connection between the Old Testament prophecies and the arrival of the Messiah. *Why John the Baptist is Important to the Christmas Story* is a timely and thought-provoking exploration of a pivotal character in the Christmas narrative. In *How to Overcome Spiritual Fatigue and Rekindle Your Passion for God*, Anurag addresses a critical issue that many individuals face in their spiritual journeys. Drawing from biblical wisdom and his own experiences, Anurag skillfully navigates the challenges of maintaining spiritual vitality in a world filled with distractions and demands. I wholeheartedly recommend this book to anyone seeking a deeper understanding of these important issues. Anurag's unique perspective and storytelling make this book a must-read for all Christians."

Sapan Kumar, *Pastor, The Way AG Church, Chattarpur, New Delhi & Academic Dean, Assemblies of God Central Bible College, New Delhi*

"With a blend of heartfelt storytelling, practical exercises, and profound insights, "Shine from Within: Embracing the Radiance of Enlightenment" offers a roadmap to unlocking your true potential and embracing the best version of yourself. This book is a radiant guide towards self-discovery, and I believe it has the power to change lives."

Dr. Kislay Kumar Singh, *Assistant Professor, Dr. Bhim Rao Ambedkar College, University of Delhi*

"What sets this book apart is its genuine authenticity. Anurag Paul doesn't rely on empty promises or quick fixes; instead, he guides you towards lasting change by encouraging you to explore your own heart. It's a refreshing departure from the one-size-fits-all approach often found in self-help books. "Shine from Within: Embracing the Radiance of Enlightenment" is a profound reminder that our imperfections are what make us beautifully human, and it empowers you to turn your vulnerabilities into strengths. I wholeheartedly endorse this book to anyone seeking a deeper connection with themselves and a more fulfilling life."

Rajiv Dua, *Chief Executive, India HIV/AIDS Alliance (Alliance India), New Delhi*

"When I first picked up this book, I couldn't help but wonder if a young author could truly navigate the complex and sensitive subjects of relationships, mental health, finance, and spirituality with the care they deserved. My initial hesitation was quickly replaced with admiration as I delved into Anurag's insightful exploration of these topics. Anurag's deft handling of these subjects is nothing short of remarkable. My initial reservations had completely dissipated by the time I reached the final chapter. This book not only addresses these crucial life areas but does so with a level of maturity and wisdom that goes beyond the author's years."

Samuel Abraham, *Marketing Communications Consultant, Bhopal*

"Life's twists and turns can leave us questioning our path, purpose, and even our existence. However, within the pages of this book, you'll find solace and wisdom that speaks to the universal challenges we all face. Anurag's ability to distil complex ideas into accessible, relatable concepts is genuinely remarkable. What sets this book apart is its universality. It doesn't matter where you are in your life's journey; the insights and guidance in its pages are applicable and relevant to all. It's a testament to the author's deep understanding of the human experience."

Rohit Jain, *Documentary Filmmaker, New Delhi*

CONTENTS

INTRODUCTION

Welcome to a journey—a profound odyssey through the intricate tapestry of the human experience. As you stand at the threshold of this book, you are about to embark on an extraordinary voyage. It is a voyage that will take you through the highs and lows of self-discovery, the nuances of relationships, the depths of mental well-being, the secrets of financial mastery, the mysteries of spirituality, and the ever-evolving landscape of our daily lives.

These 28 articles are the threads that make up this literary tapestry—a tapestry woven from the fabric of our shared experiences, our unique perspectives, and our unwavering quest for understanding and growth.

Each article is a window into a different facet of life, a mirror reflecting our aspirations, challenges, and capacity for resilience.

In the realm of self-help, you'll uncover the keys to unlocking your true potential. These articles are a roadmap, guiding you through the labyrinth of personal growth. They offer insights into building confidence, cultivating resilience, and embracing change with open arms.

As you delve into the intricacies of relationships, you'll find stories that resonate with your own experiences. These articles delve into the complexities of human connections, illuminating the path to more profound, authentic, and meaningful relationships.

Mental health is a treasure we often take for granted until it's threatened. These articles shed light on the importance of emotional well-being and offer practical strategies for navigating life's challenges. They remind us that seeking help is okay and that we're not alone in our struggles.

The wealth management chapter demystifies the finance world, offering insights into managing your money wisely and securing your financial future.

In the realms of spirituality, you'll explore the depths of your inner self. These articles encourage you to contemplate the more significant questions, to find solace in the present moment, and to seek a deeper connection with God.

Lastly, our exploration of daily interests brings you face-to-face with the world we live in. From productivity tips to health and societal issues, these articles reflect the complexity of our daily lives and offer valuable perspectives on navigating them.

But this book is not just a collection of articles—it's an invitation.

An invitation to reflect, to grow, and to evolve. It's a journey of self-discovery, a quest for wisdom, and a celebration of the human spirit.

As we embark on this journey together, I encourage you to approach each article with an open heart and mind. Let the words guide you, challenge you, and inspire you. May they provide you with the tools you need to navigate life's intricacies with grace, understanding, and an unwavering sense of purpose.

So, my dear reader, let's step into this world of exploration, insight, and transformation together. Let's embrace the tapestry of life and discover the beauty within its every thread.

Anurag Paul
New Delhi, India

FOREWORD

In a world awash with information, where voices clamour for our attention and opinions flood our screens, it's a rare and precious thing to encounter a collection of thoughts that not only resonates with our own experiences but also offers a guiding light through the labyrinth of modern existence. Anurag Paul, a member of the millennial generation, has embarked on a ten-year journey of exploration. His vessel? The written word. His compass? An innate curiosity that drives him to delve deep into the pressing questions that occupy the minds of his peers.

As we embark on this voyage through the pages of "Shine From Within: Embracing the Radiance of Enlightenment," we are reminded of King Solomon's timeless wisdom: "By wisdom, a house is built." The act of constructing a house, much like the act of writing articles and compiling them into a book, is an investment of time and resources. It demands a compelling reason, a "why," that drives us forward. So, why does it make sense to bring together these musings, originally scattered across podcasts and articles, into the cohesive tapestry of this book?

To answer that question, let us first take a brief survey of the intellectual terrain that Anurag Paul invites us to explore. "Shine from Within: Embracing the Radiance of Enlightenment" is a treasure trove of insights organized under six thematic headings, each a reflection of the intricate tapestry of our lives.

In "The Art of Relationships," Anurag guides us through the ever-evolving dance of love and human connection. He explores the phases of love, the intricacies of online dating, the nuances of communication, and the art of letting go. It's a journey through the landscape of the heart, where we nod in recognition and pause for introspection.

"Mental Wellness Explored" ventures into the depths of our minds. In an era where overthinking is a silent epidemic, Anurag offers solace and advice. He sheds light on loneliness that haunts our hyperconnected lives, reminding us that we are not alone in our struggles.

"Self-Help Unveiled" mirrors our individual and collective journeys toward self-discovery and growth. Anurag's reflections on the COVID-19 pandemic, the power of music, and conflict resolution are beacons of guidance in a world often shrouded in uncertainty.

"Mastering Wealth Management" takes us on a journey of financial literacy, a subject rarely discussed in the open. Anurag's insights provide a roadmap for wise money management.

"The Path to Spiritual Fulfillment" challenges us to explore the depths of our faith and spirituality. It's an invitation to trust, reflect on Christmas traditions, and confront spiritual fatigue. Anurag's words become a companion on our own spiritual journeys.

"Addressing Everyday Concerns" is a conversation about the changing landscape of gender roles, lessons from health crises, and the importance of gender equity. Anurag's reviews of films and shows are not mere critiques but mirrors reflecting societal narratives.

Now, we return to the question posed earlier: Is this book worthwhile, needed, or useful?

Firstly, "Shine from Within: Embracing the Radiance of Enlightenment" serves as a bridge between generations. Baby boomers and millennials alike will discover common ground in these pages. We recognize youth's enduring struggles while acknowledging the digital age's unique challenges.

Secondly, these articles are a beacon of hope, a lifeline to those navigating complex life circumstances. Anurag's genuine intent to encourage, inspire, and offer hope shines through every word. This is a beacon of unwavering optimism in a world often characterized by cynicism.

Thirdly, this book is not a rigid how-to manual but a canvas for meaningful discussions. It invites dialogue between parents and children, grandparents and grandchildren, students and teachers, and friends. Anurag's words become the catalyst for debates that lead to personal growth and collective understanding.

"Shine from Within" is a needed, worthwhile, and valuable addition to our literary landscape. It is a testament to the power of words, a source of wisdom and guidance, and an opportunity for readers to embark on their own journeys of self-discovery and transformation. Anurag Paul's work reminds us that, in a world full of noise, there is profound beauty in the written word and deep meaning in our shared human experiences. So, dear reader, embark on this journey, let these words illuminate your path, and may you find your own brilliance as you "Shine from Within."

Paul Thomson

SECTION 1
THE ART OF RELATIONSHIPS

NAVIGATING LOVE'S PHASES: KEY FOR BUILDING LASTING CONNECTION

Picture this: you meet someone, and suddenly, your heart is a symphony of fireworks. Laughter fills the air, butterflies fly in your stomach, and everything feels perfect. Ah, the honeymoon phase! Remember that enchanting period when you're building a unique connection, having the time of your life, and experiencing sheer, pure happiness? It's like the first breathtaking chapter of your love story. But much like the pages of a captivating book, this chapter eventually comes to a close.

But don't bother! As the initial lightning subsides and reality steps in, you might find yourselves entering what's often referred to as the "differences" phase. This is the stage where you begin to notice the charming features that make each of you one-of-a-kind—the traits, the habits, and all those particular nuances that define you as individuals.

And you know what? This is perfectly normal! Embracing these differences adds spice to your relationship, infusing it with vibrancy and richness.

Now, let's shift our focus to the "struggle" phase. I won't sugarcoat it; this might not be the most enjoyable part of the journey. This is where disagreements can arise, often stemming from aspects of your lives that existed long before you met each other. Echoes of past experiences might resurface. However, there's a silver lining—the "repair" phase awaits, ready to guide you through.

Imagine the "repair" phase as an opportunity to mend things together. It's similar to fixing up rough patches in a beautiful wall hanging. But let's be honest, it's not a walk in the park. It requires thoughtful consideration, open-hearted conversations, and, yes, effort. Effort is like the secret ingredient that's needed for every step of this journey.

Talk It Out: When navigating a rough patch, creating a safe space for honest communication is crucial. Sit down together and have an open conversation. Listen actively to each other's viewpoints without interruption. Remember, this isn't about assigning blame; it's an opportunity to gain insight into your partner's perspective. Sharing your thoughts openly nurtures understanding and empathy, laying the foundation for finding common ground.

Seek Compromise: Disagreements are a natural part of any relationship. The key lies in your approach. Rather than viewing disagreements as battles to win, see them as opportunities for collaboration. Seeking compromise shifts the focus from proving a point to uncovering solutions that benefit both of you.

As we've explored these practical tips, remember that effort acts as the adhesive holding your relationship together.

It's about communicating effectively, forgiving each other, and embracing the imperfections that make us all uniquely human. It's about drawing closer, building trust, and understanding that perfection isn't the goal—it's about finding someone perfectly aligned with you.

Regular Check-Ins: In the hastiness of life, it's easy to lose sight of your partner's emotional state. That's why setting aside dedicated moments for check-ins is essential. Think of it as a heartfelt conversation where you ask, "How are you doing?" These regular check-ins create a space to share emotions, thoughts, and experiences.

Show Appreciation: In the hustle of daily life, it's all too easy to overlook the efforts your partner invests in the relationship. But expressing genuine appreciation can be a game-changer. A heartfelt "thank you" or acknowledging the little things your partner does can go a long way in nurturing your connection.

And what lies ahead after navigating these phases? The "enduring love" phase! This is where you've faced challenges together, emerging stronger than ever. Your love matures into an unbreakable bond, ready to stand firm against life's trials.

But our journey doesn't end here. Let's delve into a couple more practical tips that can elevate your relationship journey to new heights.

Celebrate Milestones: The power of celebrating your journey can't be underestimated. Whether it's a milestone anniversary or a spontaneous "just because" moment, take the time to acknowledge and celebrate your accomplishments together. These moments of reflection reinforce the journey you've embarked on and the growth you've achieved.

Embrace Growth: Remember, personal growth ignites relationship growth. Support each other's aspirations and celebrate each other's victories. Your individual development adds depth to your shared journey.

Let your partner know you're ready to stand together, unwavering and steadfast, as you continue writing your love story's beautiful chapters.

SWIPE RIGHT: FINDING LOVE AND HAPPINESS IN THE DIGITAL AGE

Let's discuss one of dating apps' most important and controversial aspects: swiping left or right. You may know how it works if you've ever used a dating app like Tinder, Bumble, or Hinge. These apps show you a series of profiles with photos and a short bio, and then you can swipe left or right on them to show your interest or disinterest. If you and another person swipe right on each other's profiles, you have a match and can start chatting. But how do you decide who to swipe left or right on? What are the factors that influence your choice? And what are the consequences of swiping too much or too little? These are some of the questions we will discuss in this article.

First of all, let's talk about why people use dating apps in the first place. People use these apps mainly because of curiosity, entertainment, social validation, and finding a romantic partner. Of course, different people may have different motivations and expectations when using dating apps, which may affect how they swipe. For example, some people may swipe right on everyone they see, hoping to get as many matches as possible. This strategy is sometimes called "swiping for validation" or "swiping for ego boost." It may make you feel good in the short term, but it can also have adverse effects in the long term.

You may end up with many matches you're not interested in or compatible with. This can lead to frustration, disappointment, ghosting, or even harassment. You may miss out on some potential matches you would have liked if you had paid more attention to their profiles. This can lead to regret, missed opportunities, or even loneliness.

On the other hand, some people may swipe left on almost everyone they see, hoping to find only the best matches possible. This strategy is sometimes called "swiping for perfection" or "swiping for quality". Let's talk about some red flags you should watch out for. Some signs indicate that someone may not be a good match for you or may have ulterior motives or bad intentions. Here are some examples of red flags that you should swipe left on:

If someone asks for your phone number or personal email address before getting to know you, that's a red flag. They may be trying to scam, stalk, or take the conversation to a more intimate level without your consent.

If someone says that they are looking for someone who doesn't take themselves too seriously, that's a red flag. They may not be serious about dating, have low self-esteem, or make offensive jokes and dismiss your feelings.

If someone has too many shirtless or revealing photos, that's a red flag. They may only be interested in hookups, narcissistic, or have nothing else to offer besides their looks.

If someone does not respect your boundaries online, that's a red flag. They may be pushy, controlling, or manipulative. For example, if they try to move the conversation off the dating app, follow or friend you on another platform, or pressure you to meet up or send nudes without your consent.

They may be arrogant, entitled, or playing games. They may also have unrealistic expectations or standards for their matches. If someone uses the phrase "I don't usually swipe right, so if we match, you're pretty lucky" or something similar, that's a red flag.

These are just some red flags you should be aware of when swiping on dating apps. Of course, other red flags may be specific to your situation or preferences. Trusting your intuition and being careful about who you swipe right on is important. Remember, swiping right is not a commitment but an invitation to get to know someone better.

When swiping on dating apps, being selective and open to potential matches is important. So swipe right on people who deserve your time and attention.

So, what's the best way to swipe on dating apps? There's no definitive answer to that question, as different people may have different preferences and goals. However, here are some general tips that may help you swipe smarter and happier:

- Be clear about what you're looking for and offering on dating apps. Are you looking for something casual or serious? Are you looking for someone similar or different from you? Are you looking for someone nearby or far away? Are you looking for someone who shares your interests or challenges your views? Be honest with yourself and with others about your intentions and expectations.

- Be selective but not too picky. Don't swipe right on everyone or no one. Swipe right on people who catch your eye and spark your curiosity. Swipe left on people who don't appeal to you or raise red flags. Don't judge people solely by their looks or their bios. Give people a chance to show their personality and their values.

- Be respectful but not too polite. Don't swipe right on people just because you feel sorry for them or because you don't want to hurt their feelings. Swipe right on people because you genuinely like them or want to get to know them better. Don't swipe left on people because they're not your type or have a minor flaw. Swipe left on people because you genuinely don't like them or don't want to get to know them better.

- Be mindful but not too obsessive. Don't swipe too fast or too slow. Swipe at a pace that allows you to pay attention to each profile and make an informed decision. Don't swipe too much or too little. Swipe at a frequency that will enable you to balance your online dating life with your offline life.

THINGS YOU SHOULD NEVER SAY TO YOUR PARTNER: A GUIDE TO THE LOVING RELATIONSHIP

In any relationship, communication is vital. But there are some things that you should never say to your partner if you want to maintain a happy and healthy relationship. In this article, I will guide you about what NOT to say in a relationship and why it's essential to avoid saying these things. By understanding what not to say (and why), you can strengthen your own relationships and avoid potential conflict.

You should never say some things to your partner if you want to maintain a happy and healthy relationship. For example, "You're lucky I'm even talking to you," or "I can't believe you did that. "These kinds of phrases will only serve to create conflict and tension in your relationship. Instead, try communicating with kindness and respect, even when it's difficult. It'll make a world of difference in your relationship dynamic.

Some things are better left unsaid, and can only do harm if said. If you find yourself in a situation where tempers are flared, and words start flying, it's important to take a step back and think about what you're about to say.

In my last relationship, I can remember one particular argument where everything came to head and we said some hurtful things to each other. It felt satisfying to let all my anger out at the moment, but afterwards, I realized that those words were permanent and couldn't be taken back.

You should never threaten to leave your partner.

Why? Because you aren't communicating to resolve the underlying issues, you are simply trying to get your partner to change their behavior. The only thing threatening separation or leaving your partner will accomplish is to make them withdrawn and quiet and to avoid conflict. It will not resolve the problem, and it will likely cause you to get even less attention.

Ultimately, your partner will see you as weak and more likely to act out. Instead of trying to force your partner to change, make it clear that they can either work on the problem with you and with your help or deal with the consequences of their behavior on their own.

Don't compare your partner by saying: You are unromantic; look at them.

How do you compare? According to your age, maybe? Are you comparing yourself with them? Don't. Don't be "Unromantic". Be yourself. Be Romantic. A real Romantic. Not a fake.

Don't compete with others. It only makes you angry, depressed, and frustrated. Comparing yourself to others will never help you. The moment you are doing that, you have lost the battle. It is like telling them: I am not good enough for me.

Don't pretend you are something that you are not.

Those who compare their failures with others' successes will have many failures.

Never act with a Superiority Complex with your partner.

It's an easy recipe for disaster. When you feel this emotion, it's often dangerous. But it can also be funny, as long as it is kept light-hearted. Never treat your partner with disrespect because of their inability to dominate you. This type of behavior is toxic, not only because it will bring you an ultimate failure but because it can really hurt the partner you are trying to dominate. Don't be a control freak. It is such a turnoff and will lead to nothing good. We have to take the same care and effort in understanding our partners as we do for ourselves.

Listen and listen some more.

We all have heard a million times that the art of communication is communicating without actually speaking.

A relationship needs sharing and listening to each other.

While you may be great, your partner must know that you are also aware they are great. While you must show some competitive spirit, it is not a game of one-upmanship. It's unique, and that's what makes it attractive for you and for them. While you may be great, your partner must know that you are also aware they are great.

Never try to show that you are a perfect partner, as it is almost impossible to be one. It is advised not to make promises which you cannot keep or which can't be fulfilled. It is not appreciated in any relationship.

Don't be a 'know-it-all' person. Don't think you are always right.

Avoid complaining about your partner to others. It will only create negativity and make you look mean-spirited. Don't Treat your partner as a doormat. You do not always come first; your partner has needs too.

Never give up on your partner.

CHOOSING LOVE IN MARRIAGE

Marriage isn't just a one-time event; it's an ongoing journey of love, commitment, and growth. It's waking up every morning and consciously loving your partner despite their flaws.

To many, love is often associated with grand gestures, butterflies in the tummy, and those magical moments that make our hearts race. But love is so much more than that. As we grow older, we understand that love is not solely a feeling; it's an act of the will.

As children, love was portrayed in fairy tales and Disney movies as a happily-ever-after ending. But the reality is that love extends beyond our romantic notions as kids. It's about building a deep connection with someone, understanding their flaws, and still choosing to accept and cherish them.

When we meet someone, and those initial sparks fly, it's easy to get caught up in the whirlwind of emotions. We crave their presence, their companionship, and the joy they bring to our lives. But it's important to recognize that these feelings are just the beginning—a starting point for something greater.

Marriage is a choice—an intentional decision to spend the rest of your life with someone. It's not based solely on circumstances or motivations; it's about accepting another person, for better or worse, and sticking together through thick and thin.

Yet, we all know that life doesn't always go as planned. Challenges arise, and the flaws and imperfections of both partners come to the surface. It's during these moments that the true essence of love is revealed.

The longevity of a marriage doesn't depend solely on the strength of the initial "feelings" of love. Lasting marriages thrive because partners actively keep loving each other, even when things get tough.

It's difficult to continue loving someone despite their mistakes, irritations, and shortcomings. We see each other's weaknesses and moments of ugliness, but it's in these moments that love becomes real.

When we stand before witnesses, exchanging vows, we don't fully know the person we're committing to. But as the days, months, and years go by, we understand each other more deeply. We witness their failures, their regrets, and their struggles—and still, we choose to love them.

Marriage is a journey of growth and change. It's about navigating the ups and downs of life together as a unit. We all face challenges, make mistakes, and experience moments of disappointment. But love is about offering understanding, forgiveness, and compassion, even when it's difficult.

So, my dear readers, let's explore practical steps to help couples nurture their relationships with kindness, acceptance, and compassion.

Step one is **Effective Communication**. Open and honest communication is the foundation of a healthy relationship. Take the time to listen actively to your partner, seeking to understand their perspective without judgment. Express your thoughts and feelings with kindness and respect. Remember, it's not just about talking; it's about genuinely hearing and being heard.

Step two is having **Empathy and Understanding**. Practice putting yourself in your partner's shoes. Cultivate empathy by genuinely understanding their emotions, experiences, and needs. Show empathy through validation and support, even if you don't always agree. This fosters an environment where both couples feel free to express themselves and nurtures a deeper connection.

Step three is to **Prioritize Quality Time**. In the midst of busy lives, make a conscious effort to spend quality time together. Dedicate regular date nights or activities that you both enjoy. Disconnect from distractions and focus on each other. Quality time nurtures emotional intimacy and reinforces the bond between partners.

Step four is to **Express Appreciation and Gratitude**. Take time to acknowledge and appreciate your partner's efforts and qualities. Express gratitude for the little things they do that make a difference. A sincere mention or a simple "thank you" can go a long way toward promoting happiness and enhancing the connection.

Step five is to **Practice Forgiveness**. No relationship is immune to mistakes and misunderstandings. Cultivate a forgiving attitude and be willing to let go of grudges and past hurts. Communicate openly about the issue, seek understanding, and work together toward resolution. Forgiveness allows space for healing and growth within the relationship.

Step six is to **Support Each Other's Growth.** Encourage and support each other's individual growth and personal goals. Celebrate achievements and provide a safe space for exploration and self-discovery. When both partners feel supported in their respective journeys, it enhances the overall strength of the relationship.

Step seven is to **Cultivate Intimacy and Affection.** Physical and emotional intimacy are vital components of a thriving marriage. Create moments of connection through gestures of affection, such as hugs, kisses, and gentle touches. Nurture emotional intimacy by sharing your thoughts, dreams, and vulnerabilities. Intimacy deepens the bond and creates a sense of security within the relationship.

Step eight is to **Practice Patience and Understanding.** Recognize that both partners are imperfect and will make mistakes. Cultivate patience and understanding when challenges arise. Instead of resorting to anger or blame, seek solutions together and work through difficulties with compassion and empathy.

Step nine is to **Seek Professional Help if Needed.** Always remember that seeking professional assistance is not a sign of weakness but rather a brave move toward growth. If you find yourself struggling to navigate specific challenges, consider seeking the guidance of a marriage counselor or therapist. They may offer insightful advice and helpful resources to aid in developing your relationship.

Step ten is to Practice Continual Growth and Learning. Recognize that nurturing a relationship is an ongoing journey. Stay curious and open to learning more about yourself and your partner. Explore books, workshops, or podcasts that focus on healthy relationships. Embrace personal growth and encourage your partner to do the same.

When we choose love, our partnerships grow and flourish despite the difficulties.

So, my dear readers, I want to leave you with a simple message: Choose love. Choose to embrace the imperfections and complexities of your partner and keep nurturing your relationship with kindness, acceptance, and compassion.

WHY YOUR RELATIONSHIP IS FAILING: 5 REAL REASONS RELATIONSHIPS FAIL

You think maintaining a good relationship is easy. It's not. It requires consistent effort.

Michael and Nicole have been dating each other for the last few months. Nicole often used to feel that something was failing in their relationship as a couple who were once passionately in love with each other. Both of them were clueless.

Have you ever wondered why relationships fail? There can be more than one reason, but five of them are the most common.

1. Relationships fail when you don't prioritize your partner

When you scurry through various life activities and don't have time for your partner, it is a covert signal that your partner's name is way down on your priority list. You may be a victim of busyness syndrome without even realizing it. Remember those initial dating days when your partner was always in your mind? A simple text was enough to activate all your sensory nerves.

When did you last go out for lunch or dinner with your partner?

2. You don't trust your partner anymore

The trust factor is essential for any relationship, whether romantic or professional. If you don't trust your partner for small things, it is hard even to comprehend that you will trust them for bigger things. Your partner may have failed you in the past, but that doesn't mean he/she will fail you every time in the future. There is a difference between losing trust and not trusting at all. You may find it difficult to trust your partner because of incidents that left you devastated and cheated, but completely losing trust can turn you into a maniac and you can ask for proof for everything your partner has said.

Have you ever checked your partner's phone in their absence?

3. You use your past relationships as the reference point

When you constantly dwell on the past and quote sentences like, "My girlfriend/boyfriend never did this", you have already initiated digging the graveyard of your relationship. No two human beings can be compared with each other as they have different upbringings and past experiences. Their past largely shapes the way they behave today with others.

Carrying the emotional baggage of your past relationship and dumping it on your partner can be distressing for your partner.

Do you often quote how your ex behaved in certain situations?

4. Relationships fail when you don't communicate

The foundation of any successful relationship is open, honest communication. Conveying your true feelings to your partner and not hiding them is crucial. Holding a grudge against your partner and not communicating the reason for the grudge you are keeping will not help. In the long run, avoiding direct communication can slowly harbor feelings of indifference, bitterness and withdrawal.

Do you find it challenging to convey areas of improvement to your partner?

5. Relationships fail when only one partner is making all the efforts

Suppose you are feeling exhausted and burnt out as your partner is not making any effort to continue the relationship. In that case, it is probably the beginning of the end of your relationship. Lack of affection for your partner shows up in various ways, and letting the other partner strive alone for the relationship is one of those signs. Valuing your partner irrespective of their imperfection is essential. When you work together in a relationship, there are high chances of winning.

Do you see signs of withdrawal in your relationship?

EVERYTHING I LEARNED ABOUT OVERTHINKING PARTNER

Joshua was romantically involved with his college best friend, Rebecca. Joshua was an extrovert and passionate individual with a zest for life. On the other hand, Rebecca was an introvert with an overthinking mind.

Joshua didn't want to see Rebecca unhappy at any point in time. Rebecca would spend a lot of time thinking through worst-case scenarios about their relationship. Joshua was constantly trying to make Rebecca feel supported and loved.

I have learned from experience that overthinkers tend to keep their inherent fear and apprehensions to themselves and spend a lot of time arriving at conclusions in any specific situation. There are certain non-negotiables when you are in a relationship with an overthinker.

Overthinkers can be like turmeric milk in your life- the way turmeric milk scares cold away, you can also be chased by them if you fail to understand them because overthinkers can complicate simple things by constantly pondering over them.

It is advisable to check their emotional standpoint by asking them about their well-being. An open environment should be given to your overthinker partner where they feel comfortable communicating the thoughts going on in their mind. This will help them to trust you and share their genuine feelings with you. Always let them think that they have a partner who will stand with them in the highs and lows of life.

If your partner is quiet and not communicating, they may be deep in their thoughts. You can ask them about the issue that they are thinking about. If your partner shares, try to understand them better by asking questions that will help them open up and give you a fair idea of the origin of their thoughts. Your questions will help them process their thoughts well, and your partner may appreciate that you are interested in knowing what is going on in their head. Never doubt your partner's intentions when they share their ideas or feelings with you or agree unquestioningly. If you doubt their intentions, this may trigger them to overthink about that particular issue in the future, which you would never want.

Overthinkers generally are thoughtful and like spending time in their own head by reflecting on problems and contemplating past experiences. You need to help them understand that things are not as bad as they have contemplated in their mind.

Overthinkers worry a lot about the trajectory of their relationship. Their worrying indicates they want to be prepared for the worst.

Your overthinker partner can also be investigative and observant. Never lie to them, if you do so, they will be suspicious of all your activities and statements in the coming days.

Using sarcastic jokes targeting your overthinker partner can get you in trouble. Your sarcasm can become your worst nightmare as overthinkers tend to overthink every word you have spoken to them; they can easily conclude that sarcasm has been used to belittle them.

All overthinkers know that they are dealing with the issue of overthinking. Please don't put a label on them. Don't annoy them by asking them not to overthink. Instead, help them to take baby steps to overcome this habit so that you have a healthy and fulfilling relationship.

BEING WITH SOMEONE WHO DOES NOT WANT TO LOVE YOU BUT ALSO DOES NOT WANT TO LOSE YOU

Being with someone who does not want to love you but does not want to lose you is a feeling of uncertainty rather than happiness. It is a thought that sometimes stresses the mind and makes it feel heavy. But, if we can accept our emotions as they are and attempt to understand them, then this uncertain feeling becomes something that helps us grow in life.

Sometimes, knowing if someone really wants to be with you is hard. And, unfortunately, when love looks like this, it often ends up being the worst kind of relationship: you're in more pain than anyone else.

This is one of the most challenging love situations to deal with. It is hard enough for your partner to be with you and even more complex when there are no good options regarding the relationship. While it might be possible that this may lead to some conflict, you can try to stay hopeful (and patient) throughout and strive to understand each other more fully.

Love is so much more than a feeling. It's an intense journey that takes unwavering commitment, determination, and a huge dose of trust. And this is what we all need in our lives.

Love doesn't mess around. It takes commitment, trust, and a whole lot of emotion. We could all use a little more love in our lives, whether it be a friend, family member, or even a pet.

Love is a fantastic feeling. It brings difficult-to-describe joy and happiness into our lives.

Love is never easy, but it's always worth it!

The process of falling in love is amazing. But the act of sharing a love that lasts forever is even better.

Being in a relationship where you feel uncertain and pressured but cannot leave is difficult, it's like happiness gets put on hold while you wait and hope things might improve. It's like a feeling of emptiness, a disturbing feeling that makes you lose focus and second guess if your place in the world is meaningful or not. You feel this feeling getting stronger when you are around those who take away your happiness, but it becomes weaker when you are with someone who fills your life with joy. However, if we can learn to accept our feelings as they are, we can understand what makes us feel this way and start thinking positively even through the hard times, paving the road to a more positive future.

When we accept our feelings and understand them, they become something that helps us grow.

When you are the third wheel in your relationship, love is not something that you seem to be able to get enough of. It is something that you crave but feel that it is out of reach. This feeling leaves a yearning inside you, which tends to drive you crazy when your partner ignores your desire to spend more time with them. You accept that your relationship will always be just like this, but something in you tells you that things could always change.

Emotions are powerful. They make you feel different things based on how you think. Sometimes, emotions can overwhelm you. To understand them, we must first be able to accept that they exist and figure out why we're feeling what we do.

Deep inside us, we know that how we treat people is no measure of how much they love us. If a partner treats you with respect, consideration, and kindness, this person truly cares about you.

You deserve to be treated the way you've always deserved: like someone special. And if a partner does not treat you that way, it means they aren't ready for a relationship with someone like you.

A healthy relationship is like a spring day — filled with hope, optimism, and happiness. On the other hand, an unhealthy one is just like an autumn day — cold and empty without any meaning or purpose.

A partner ignoring you means they're involved in their own world and missing out on yours. But don't let it go unresolved: If your partner ignores or does not respond, talk about it. This helps show him that you're an equal partner and have feelings, too.

It can be possible that your partner may be ignoring you because they're dealing with their own issues. It could be anything from stress from work to problems at home. Whatever it is, make sure you talk about it and not isolate yourself.

Patching things up with a loved one can be rewarding but also difficult. Don't settle for just making amends with your partner; work to mend the relationship as a whole.

HOW TO LET GO OF SOMEONE YOU STILL LOVE

If you've ever been in a relationship that ended, you know how difficult it can be to let go of someone you once loved. You might wonder if you'll ever get over them, if you'll ever find someone else and ever be happy again. You might feel stuck in the past, unable to move on.

But is it possible to stop loving someone? Is it something that we can control? Is it something that we should even want? And what does it mean to move on from someone?

We shall delve deeply into these issues and others in this article.

We will discover that love is not a simple or static thing. It's a complex and dynamic process involving our brains, hearts, and souls. It's something that can change over time, for better or for worse. It can stay with us even when the person is gone.

But we're also going to discover that love is not a prison. It's a gift. It enriches our lives, teaches us important lessons, and makes us grow as human beings. We can cherish it but also let go of it when it no longer serves us.

We will discover that moving on doesn't mean we stop loving someone. It means that we start loving ourselves more.

So join me on this journey of exploring one of the most universal and profound questions of human existence: can we ever stop loving someone?

If you've ever gone through a breakup, you know how painful it can be. You might feel like your heart is shattered like you've lost a part of yourself, as you'll never be happy again. You might cry yourself to sleep, wondering if you'll ever get over your partner. You might ask yourself: can I ever stop loving them?

Well, the answer is more complex. Because love is not a switch that you can turn on and off. Love is not something that you can erase from your memory. Love is not something that you can replace with someone else.

Love is something that changes you, that shapes you, that teaches you. Love is complex, messy, and beautiful. Love stays with you, even when the person is gone.

But that doesn't mean that you can't move on. That doesn't mean that you can't heal. That doesn't mean that you can't find love again.

There is a difference between moving on and unloving someone.

"Just because someone is gone doesn't mean that you stop loving them. You stop loving them when they stop making you happy."

Think about it for a moment. What does it mean to love someone? Is it just a feeling? Is it just a word? Or is it something more?

To me, love is not just an emotion. Love is an action. Love is a choice. Love is a commitment.

When you love someone, you don't just say it. You show it. You do things for them. You make them happy. You make them feel valued. You make them feel alive.

And when someone loves you, they do the same for you. They make you happy. They make you feel valued. They make you feel alive.

But sometimes, things change. Sometimes, people change. Sometimes, love fades.

And when that happens, when someone stops making you happy, stops showing you love, and stops being there for you, then it's time to let them go.

Because holding on to someone who doesn't love you back is unhealthy. It's not fair to yourself or them. It's not good for your mental or emotional well-being.

It's OK to acknowledge the good times you had with them. It's OK to appreciate the lessons they taught you. It's OK to cherish the memories they gave you.

It's OK to heal. It's OK to find happiness elsewhere. But it's also OK to move on.

Moving on doesn't mean that you stop loving them. It means that you start loving yourself more.

It means that you recognize your worth and your potential.

It means that you open your heart to new possibilities and new people.

It means that you find someone who makes you happy again.

Someone who adores you in the manner that you deserve.

Someone who makes you believe in the beauty of love again.

But this time, a different kind of love.

A better kind of love.

A lasting kind of love.

So yes, my friends, you can fully move on and never want to go back to your ex, but also, your heart will never truly unlove them because they once made you happy, which is OK.

And if you're heartbroken right now, I promise you, you will find love again.

You will find love again.

You will find love again.

SECTION 2
MENTAL WELLNESS EXPLORED

EVERYTHING I LEARNED ABOUT OVERTHINKING.
5 WAYS TO DEFEAT IT

I met Veronica last year. Veronica called herself an overthinker. At first, I thought she thinks a lot about life issues, and that's okay.

As our friendship developed, I observed her repeating this sentence, "Anurag, I am an overthinker. This issue is bothering me".

For me, I had this understanding that "Overthinkers" are people who think a lot. I mean the simple interpretation of the word. This understanding changed gradually as I dived deeper into this subject.

Who are overthinkers?

They overthink everything and spend a lot of time thinking about or exploring matters in a way likely to cause problems or have adverse consequences. Overthinkers are not only highly conscious of their thoughts but also devote a lot of time trying to understand the origins, meaning, and aftereffects of their thoughts, which keeps flowing round and round inside their mind.

Overthinkers often question their own thought process. They tend to struggle or might have a low tolerance for unprompted and uninvited thoughts, which they are aware of and even sometimes know that these thoughts will not bring any favorable results.

Overthinkers think about the worst things that can happen, and they can get stuck in indecision, which means they find it very difficult to make decisions, even the simplest ones. Overthinkers can think about the labor pain and discomfort that pregnancy can bring, leading them to stall and not even plan a baby.

Are overthinkers toxic?

Overthinkers can turn out to be toxic in a relationship as they might think that they are working on an issue, but not only does overthinking not produce solutions, it also worsens the problem. It's a fact that overthinking consumes the time and energy a particular individual could utilize to solve a problem. Overthinking deeply impairs problem solving abilities, which makes it difficult to take tangible actions on a possible solution, and these individuals can become more pessimistic about the future.

Overthinkers can easily drive their partners away in a relationship. Overthinkers may reach out for help more often, but they tend to share their unhappiness to the point of being infuriating.

How do people react to overthinkers?

Initially, people around might be sympathetic, but after a while, they might get irritated when overthinkers seem never to take visible steps to solve problems, even if you listen to them attentively and give constructive feedback or advice. People can lead an overthinker to a solution, but it completely depends on them whether they will take steps towards the solution or not.

Five ways to overcome the habit of overthinking

1. Look at things from a different point of view

Looking at the world from a different point of view can help overthinkers. They need to remember that their emotions can interfere with their ability to look at situations objectively. Taking a step back and looking at the evidence can help them analyze whether that particular thought is true or not. This in turn can make them productive by looking at the bigger picture.

2. Live in the present

Dwelling on the past does not help at all. For people who are overthinkers, overthinking can become such a chronic habit that they cannot even make out when they are doing it. Living in the present without worrying about the past hurts and experiences can prove to be helpful. Turning away from past bad experiences, rather than focusing on what could have been done, focusing on what could be done and trying to come to a conclusion to solve the problem by living in the present can help an overthinker.

3. Focus on being kind to yourself

Self-acceptance and being kind to themselves can be the key for an overthinker. Any self-demeaning thought should be avoided and embracing fear can go a long way toward limiting the habit of overthinking.

4. Keep a journal of your accomplishments

Overthinkers have to consciously adopt new ways to stay away from the habit of overthinking. Keeping a journal/notebook to jot down accomplishments from the past week or month can help them understand and cherish their success. These entries in the journal can help them reflect and learn how to understand themselves, serve & forgive others, and move toward their close ones rather than staying away.

5. Seek help

As humans, we may have thoughts constantly running inside our minds throughout the day, which is normal. Some thoughts about one situation can overlap with thoughts about another situation or incident, but when people go back over and over again to the ones that stimulate strong emotions, it can turn into overthinking. A very small section of people can successfully classify their thoughts concretely so that they do not turn to overthinking. But a majority of people will eventually engage in overthinking in one situation or another. Overthinkers don't have to go alone on their journey towards overcoming this habit. Seeking outside help from a qualified therapist is advisable if this trait is becoming unbearable.

THE LONELINESS PHENOMENON: UNDERSTANDING HIKIKOMORI IN JAPAN

A new government survey revealed that nearly 1.5 million people in Japan have withdrawn from society, leading secluded lives within the confines of their homes. These individuals, known as hikikomori, are defined by the government as those who have isolated themselves for at least six months, with some barely leaving their bedrooms. Some of them only go out to buy groceries or for occasional activities.

Let's first delve into the story of Emi. Emi was once a vibrant and outgoing young woman with dreams of pursuing a career in the arts. However, as the pressures of societal expectations and academic achievements grew, she found herself overwhelmed and anxious. The stress only intensified when she entered the competitive job market after graduation.

Unable to cope with the mounting pressure, Emi slowly withdrew from her friends and family. She stopped attending social events and even stopped going to work. Her world shrank to the confines of her small apartment, and the outside world became an intimidating and frightening place.

Months turned into years, and Emi's social circle dwindled to zero. She occasionally stepped out to buy groceries, but even that became daunting. Instead, she found solace in her bedroom, where she immersed herself in the virtual world of video games and online communities.

Emi's parents were apprehensive about their daughter's sudden isolation, but every attempt to reach out to her was met with resistance and frustration. The distance between them grew, leaving Emi feeling misunderstood and her parents feeling helpless.

Eventually, Emi's family sought professional help. With the support of a therapist, she began to address the underlying anxiety and depression that had led to her hikikomori state. It was a slow and challenging journey, but gradually, Emi started venturing outside her home with the guidance of her therapist. She attended group therapy sessions to interact with others facing similar challenges.

Over time, Emi regained her confidence and started exploring her artistic passions once more. While the road to recovery was arduous, her story is a testament to the transformative power of understanding and compassionate support.

Emi's life story serves as a tender reminder of the actual impact hikikomori can have on individuals and their loved ones. The path to recovery may be challenging, but with empathy, understanding, and support, there is hope for a brighter future.

The phrase "hikikomori" was coined back in the 1980s, and authorities have been increasingly concerned about the issue over the past decade. But the pandemic has added fuel to the fire, as a survey conducted last November by the government's Children and Families Agency indicated that COVID-19 has become a significant factor in their reclusive lifestyle. A staggering one-fifth of respondents cited the pandemic as a key reason for their social isolation.

It is important to consider the pandemic's effects. Japan, like many other nations in East Asia, implemented rigorous pandemic regulations until 2022, even as other nations adopted a "living with Covid" approach. The reduced opportunities for contact with other people during this prolonged period likely contributed to the worsening of existing social problems like loneliness, isolation, and financial hardship.

Experts have linked hikikomori to psychological issues such as depression and anxiety, but societal factors, including Japan's patriarchal norms and demanding work culture, also play a significant role. The country's aging population and population crisis add to the complexity of this issue, as the elderly population swells while the birth rate declines.

This creates a double challenge for families with hikikomori members, known as the "8050 problem," where social recluses in their 50s rely on parents in their 80s. Authorities have been striving to address this issue and provide support through various services, including consultations, home visits, and community outreach efforts.

But as the pandemic progressed, the problems grew more serious, prompting the government to study loneliness nationally in 2021 and provide a more thorough countermeasures plan in December 2022. These measures include public awareness campaigns, suicide prevention initiatives through social media, additional school counselors and social workers, and a 24/7 phone consultation service for those with weak social ties.

There are also specific programs to support single-parent households, such as meal plans for their children, housing loans, and planning services for those going through divorce. While the pandemic may have amplified feelings of loneliness and isolation, it has also brought to light pre-existing problems that often go unnoticed.

As Japan's single-person and elderly single-person households are expected to increase in the future, the government needs to address the underlying issues of loneliness and isolation inherent in Japanese society.

Understanding the psychological factors that contribute to hikikomori

Hikikomori is often linked to psychological issues such as depression, anxiety, and social anxiety disorder. These individuals tend to withdraw from society due to the overwhelming stress and pressure they experience in various aspects of their lives. Japan's competitive and demanding work culture and societal expectations can take a toll on their mental health, leading them to seek solace in isolation.

The pandemic has been challenging for everyone, but it has hit hikikomori particularly hard. With reduced opportunities for social interaction and increased anxiety about the virus, many individuals who were already struggling with isolation found it even more challenging to engage with the outside world. The pandemic heightened their fears and reinforced their inclination to stay secluded.

Families and communities must provide understanding and support without judgment. Encouraging open communication and seeking professional help, such as therapy and counselling, can make a significant difference. By encouraging welcoming and sympathetic environments, the stigma associated with mental health issues and social reclusiveness can be minimised.

It is crucial to spread knowledge about hikikomori and endeavor to build an understanding and caring society.

If you or someone you know is struggling with feelings of isolation or loneliness, we need not forget that asking for assistance is a sign of strength. Reach out to friends, family, or mental health professionals. Remember, you are not alone.

SECTION 3
SELF-HELP UNVEILED

EMBRACING SELF-LOVE

For many of us, loving ourselves can seem impossible, as negative self-talk, shame, and fear can prevent us from showing ourselves the compassion we deserve. We often have high expectations of ourselves, yet we can love and accept our friends and family members for who they are, even when they are not at their best.

First and foremost, it's essential to understand that there is nothing wrong with you. The thoughts that create a story around your sense of self-worth are not a mirror of reality but rather a faulty wiring in your neural pathways that were created due to your life experiences. The mind-body connection is powerful, and many issues we tend to beat ourselves up for come down to a dysregulated nervous system. Knowing this, we can begin healing our mind-body connection and reprogramming our brains.

Even the decision to prioritize your healing journey is an act of selflove, so if you have started on this path, you are already moving in the right direction. Here are some steps to help you continue on your journey toward self-love:

Respond to your inner critic. Write out all of your criticisms of yourself, then make a strong, bold response. WHAT THEN? Then, as if a close friend had come to you with this issue, write a compassionate response. Embrace that anger! Your inner critic should be reminded that you are trying your best. Maintain this routine no matter what arises, whether it is an internal event or a journaling routine.

Forgive yourself. Say, "I'm sorry," to yourself as you embrace yourself. One of the most important steps on the road to self-love is forgiving ourselves for all of the bad decisions we make out of fear or shame, the things we have done to others, and how we have treated ourselves.

Take a look at your social media feeds. Make sure the social media profiles you follow are run by real people who live realistic lives. Unfollow the accounts if they make you feel uninspired and underwhelmed. Follow those who are positive influences and are concerned about global issues.

Find a friendly community. It's challenging to try to love oneself by yourself. Join a club, organization, or team so you can experience the satisfying feelings of being a member of a welcoming community. There is a tribe someplace for whatever interests you.

Find the movement medicine. Finding a movement routine that makes you feel good is a big step towards getting to know your body, not just for what it looks like but also for what it can do. Try out various activities until you find something that makes you feel like you have returned to your body, such as sports, exercises, gyms, running routes, or musical genres to dance to.

Remember, the path to self-love is not linear, but as long as you offer yourself compassion daily, your self-love will only grow, and so much good stuff will follow. Embracing self-love is a journey worth taking, and it all starts with you.

Finally, it's essential to surround yourself with positive influences. This could be supportive friends and family members, inspirational books or podcasts, or even affirmations and positive self-talk. By surrounding yourself with positivity, you can shift your mindset towards self-love and acceptance.

THREE THINGS I LEARNED ABOUT MATURE PEOPLE

aturity can be seen as the process of becoming better, more skilled, more knowledgeable, or more sophisticated. This is often a sign of growth and development.

Maturity is often used to refer to a person's feelings and thoughts when they are faced with certain situations. So, it is said that a person has reached his/her maturity level when they have thought through problems and feels capable of handling them.

Some people mature faster than others, but in general, most people reach maturity by age 25. When this happens, the person becomes more confident about themselves and their ability to handle things.

I have observed that there are three common signs of mature people:

1. Mature people no longer complain about how life is unfair

People who are not mature tend to develop an attitude of complaining. This is because they can't imagine their life without complaining. It becomes an integral part of their life to the point where it has become a habit. They use it every time they are faced with a situation that makes them frustrated or when they feel unheard. Their complaining attitude makes sure that they do not let their emotions get in the way of acting on things and instead it lets them out by complaining to someone who will listen.

When you are mature, you find that you are happier with your life and less likely to complain about what is unfair or wrong.

You start to feel gratitude for the things in your life that others would complain about. You feel grateful for your loved ones, friends, and even strangers willing to help you when needed. You start to see the good in everything and realize how lucky you are compared to those who don't have anything.

A lot of people tend to complain because they think it will help them get what they want. But what these people don't realize is that by complaining, they're just worsening their situation because no one wants to work or be in a relationship with someone who constantly complains.

With fewer complaints, everyone wins.

2. Mature people fix problems on their own

When it comes to maturity, self-reliance is the answer. If you want to be mature, you need to be able to do your work independently and still do well. You must have the self-reliance skills that will help you in different situations.

Fixing your problems on your own can be a good thing. It gives you a sense of accomplishment and strengthens your self-worth. However, some people struggle with the idea of solving their problems because they always want to avoid responsibility, avoid feeling guilty, and so on.

Some people don't take care of their problems on their own. When they know that there are people out there who can help them, they avoid taking the first step and opt for someone to do the work for them. There is an essential lesson in self-reliance, which we all have to learn at some point — that there are no shortcuts in life.

3. Mature people stay calm when things don't go according to plan

We should not strive for perfection. That's not always possible; even if it is, it's too narrow a goal. And when we keep calm in difficult situations and take one step at a time instead of getting overwhelmed, we achieve more than we would have otherwise.

Maturity shows people how they can handle difficult situations such as work-related stress or pressure. The general advice is to keep calm and composed in any way possible. Staying calm is important for anyone dealing with a demanding set of responsibilities at work or home because they help you stay focused on tasks that need your attention.

Being composed and keeping a clear head is essential for success. One of the most important skills found in a mature person is to have the ability to stay calm and composed in the face of adversity.

It's not easy to stay calm when things don't go according to plan. Staying composed is rare, and we must use strength and effort to maintain our composure in trying circumstances. But staying calm is necessary for different sets of situations in life that we come across. When you are feeling frustrated or stressed during a difficult time, take care of yourself by regaining control, which can be tried by taking deep breaths. Try not to react too quickly; give your mind time to process what is happening. Take solace in knowing that others have been through what you are going through now.

2020 – A YEAR OF SELF-REFLECTION DURING THE PANDEMIC

I reflect on the unprecedented year of 2020, which changed everything. While the world struggled with uncertainty, fear, and isolation, I found myself on a journey of deep self-reflection. What began as a time of worry and anxiety ultimately became an opportunity for growth, healing, and transformation. In sharing this, I hope that you may find encouragement, comfort, and tools for your journey through life's challenges.

Facing the Unknown

When the pandemic hit, none of us knew what the next day would hold. Like many, I asked, "Will I have financial security next month? What will happen to the global economy? Will I have enough resources to fulfill my life's dreams?" These questions weighed heavily on me, creating a sense of helplessness and anxiety. The uncertainties of life were magnified, and I, too, was affected by this global crisis.

However, uncertainty is not something new to the human experience. It's simply that we had never faced it on such a global scale. The pandemic forced us to confront our fears and reevaluate what truly mattered. As I pondered these questions, I realized that security doesn't come from external circumstances but from within. The moment I shifted my focus from what I couldn't control to what I could — my mindset, habits, and inner peace — I began reclaiming a sense of stability.

The Emotional Rollercoaster

During those months of staying home, I became more sensitive than usual. I found myself being hyper-critical, quick to point out what was wrong in the world. The stress of isolation and uncertainty magnified my anxieties and frustrations. I would critique myself, the people around me, and the world at large. I became trapped in a cycle of negativity.

Acknowledging how much our emotional state can affect our perspective is important. In these moments, we must show ourselves grace. After all, who could navigate such uncharted waters without feeling the strain? My tendency to criticize was not a failure but a signal that something within needed healing. It reminded me that my inner turmoil was a call to work on myself to grow emotionally, spiritually, and mentally.

The Power of Choice

Despite my awareness that life comes with challenges, I realized that I was not fully embracing the opportunity that hardship brings. We often wait for life to change before we change ourselves, but the reverse is true: transformation begins with us. I understood that while I could not change the external circumstances of the pandemic, I could change how I responded to them.

Change is a decision. It's not enough to desire change; we must take actionable steps. During the pandemic, I reflected on my priorities, values, and mindset. I began to shed the layers of negativity and adopt a mindset rooted in faith and positivity. This shift didn't happen overnight, but as I consistently worked on it, I saw glimpses of peace returning to my life.

Strength Through Connection

One of my most transformative decisions was reconnecting with friends and family. Isolation can lead us to retreat inward, but it's in times of solitude that we most need the support of others. I reached out to friends I hadn't spoken to in years, and one of them organized a virtual reunion with my old college group. That simple act of connection was like a breath of fresh air, a reminder that we are not alone in our struggles.

There is power in sharing our burdens. It reminds us that while our pain may be personal, it is also universal. We are all navigating this life together, and the support we give and receive is a lifeline that sustains us during the darkest moments.

Letting Go of the Old

One of the most significant realizations I had during this time of reflection was that I was clinging to old patterns and ways of thinking. I had to let go of what no longer served me. Holding on to negativity, fear, and past failures only perpetuates them. Life is like a mirror — we receive what we give out. If we put out fear and doubt, that's what we attract back. We open the door to possibilities if we put out hope and faith.

Letting go of the past doesn't mean forgetting it or pretending it didn't happen. It means freeing ourselves from the grip of regret and moving forward with wisdom. As I released old patterns, I felt a weight lift off my shoulders. I began to focus on what I could build in the present rather than what I had lost in the past.

Moving Forward with Hope

As I move forward into the future, I carry with me a renewed sense of confidence. Yes, there are still challenges, and the pandemic is not entirely behind us, but I've learned to trust in the goodness around me and within me. Where there was once fear, I now hold onto peace. I've chosen to believe that better days are ahead, not because I ignore reality but because I know that hope is a powerful force.

I've always been a dreamer, and the events of 2020 haven't changed that. If anything, they've made my dreams stronger and more purposeful. I dream big about my relationships, my career, and my faith. I know that setbacks are not the end but simply a stepping stone to something greater. In this journey of life, failure is not final unless we allow it to be.

Encouragement for Your Journey

If there's one thing I want you to take away from my experience, it's this: Growth happens in the most unlikely places. The moments that seem the hardest are often the ones that shape us the most. You don't need to have all the answers or know exactly what the future holds. You need faith in the process and trust in the growth that's happening inside of you.

As you move forward, be kind to yourself. Take time for self-reflection, but don't dwell in the past. Let go of what no longer serves you, and embrace the possibility of change. Surround yourself with people who lift you up, and most importantly, choose to believe in your capacity to overcome and thrive.

2020 was a year of self-reflection, but it was also a year of preparation. As we step into the future, let's do so with hearts full of hope, knowing that the best is yet to come.

EVERYTHING YOU NEED TO KNOW ABOUT THE POWER OF MUSIC

Music has always been a powerful force in our lives, whether it's a favorite song that brings back cherished memories, an energetic tune that gets us moving, or a soothing melody that helps us relax. I've realized that music entertains us and holds an incredible capacity for healing and transformation. It can affect our emotions, influence our physical state, and even serve as a tool for personal growth. In this article, we'll dive deeper into the power of music, exploring how it can improve both our mental and physical health and guide us toward a more balanced and fulfilling life.

Music as a Catalyst for Emotional Well-being

Music is a deeply personal experience. For some, it's a soundtrack to their daily lives; for others, it represents moments of connection with friends, family, or even complete strangers. This shared experience is one of music's greatest strengths — it can evoke a range of emotions that connect us to ourselves and others.

For example, think about how a particular song can transport you to a specific time and place. A love song might remind you of a relationship, or an upbeat track might take you back to a carefree summer. These emotional connections are powerful because they provide comfort, joy, and healing.

Scientific studies have consistently shown that listening to music releases dopamine, the "feel-good" neurotransmitter associated with pleasure and reward. This explains why a simple song can elevate your mood, reduce anxiety, and combat feelings of sadness or loneliness. By tapping into these emotions, music allows us to express feelings we might otherwise struggle to articulate.

Emotional Rescue Through Music

A close friend of mine recently shared how music helped him during a period of profound grief. After losing a loved one, he found it difficult to express his emotions. One day, while driving, he came across a song that perfectly encapsulated his sadness. Listening to that song became a cathartic experience, allowing him to release the tears he had been holding back. It helped him find the words he couldn't speak, and slowly, he began to heal. This story illustrates how music can become a lifeline, offering emotional relief during life's most challenging moments.

Music as a Mental and Physical Stimulant

Music doesn't just make us feel good emotionally — it also directly impacts our bodies. When we listen to music, our brainwaves synchronize with the rhythm, creating different states of consciousness. For example, slow, calming music induces alpha waves, which promote relaxation, while faster, upbeat music can stimulate beta waves, boosting focus and alertness.

This is why music is often used in various settings to enhance productivity or elevate physical performance. The right music can enhance cognitive and physical abilities, whether it's a fast-paced playlist to push through a workout or a soft background tune while studying.

Boosting Productivity

I recall a period when I was working on a particularly challenging writing project. I was struggling to focus, my mind wandering, and my motivation waning. Then I decided to put on instrumental music — something light and not too distracting. Almost immediately, I felt a shift. The music helped me maintain my focus for longer stretches, and I became more immersed in my work. Music has the ability to do this by engaging our brains and creating an optimal environment for concentration and creativity.

In fitness, music plays an equally powerful role. Athletes and fitness enthusiasts often rely on high-energy music to push through tough workouts. Studies have shown that music can increase endurance, help regulate breathing, and improve overall physical performance. By syncing your movements to the beat of the music, you naturally become more efficient and engaged in the activity.

Music as a Tool for Stress Relief and Healing

In a world filled with stress, music offers an accessible and effective means of reducing tension. Hospitals and healthcare facilities have long recognized the therapeutic potential of music, incorporating it into treatment programs for patients. Music therapy has been shown to lower blood pressure, reduce pain, and promote relaxation, all of which aid in faster recovery from illnesses and surgeries.

One fascinating aspect of music therapy is its ability to help the body release endorphins — natural painkillers produced by the brain. By focusing the mind on music, patients can experience relief from physical discomfort, often requiring fewer pain medications as a result.

I recently read about a cancer patient who found solace in music during her treatment. The physical and emotional toll of chemotherapy left her drained and anxious. However, when her healthcare team introduced music therapy, she found an unexpected source of strength. Listening to soft, calming music during treatments helped ease her anxiety and gave her a sense of control over her emotional state. Over time, she noticed a significant reduction in her stress levels, which in turn contributed to a more positive outlook on her recovery.

Music therapy is beneficial not only in medical settings but also in other settings. It can be a simple yet powerful tool to manage stress in everyday life. Whether you're feeling overwhelmed by work or going through a personal crisis, taking a few minutes to listen to calming music can significantly reduce stress and create a sense of inner peace.

Music as a Path to Self-Expression

Self-expression is vital to human well-being, and music provides a unique outlet for that. Whether you're playing an instrument, singing along to your favorite song, or simply listening to music that resonates with you, you're engaging in self-expression. This can be incredibly freeing, especially for those struggling to express themselves through words.

Through music, we can explore different facets of our personality, tap into our creativity, and communicate emotions that might otherwise remain unspoken. This is particularly important for people who have experienced trauma or emotional hardships, as music offers a way to process and release these feelings.

A Personal Journey in Music

Growing up, my family was deeply connected to Bollywood music. My parents adored the legendary Mohammed Rafi; his songs always played in our home. I didn't realize it at the time, but these early musical experiences shaped my emotional landscape. As I got older, I developed my own musical tastes, but I often returned to the songs of my childhood when I needed comfort or inspiration. Music became a way to express my identity and connect with my roots.

Exploring Different Genres for Maximum Benefit

One of the most exciting aspects of music is its diversity. Whether you're drawn to classical compositions, rock anthems, or soulful ballads, each genre brings its own unique benefits. Classical music, for instance, is known for its calming effects, making it an excellent choice for relaxation or meditation. On the other hand, light rock or pop can boost your mood and even improve decision-making by creating an upbeat atmosphere.

The key is to explore different types of music and find what resonates with you. There's no one-size-fits-all when it comes to the healing power of music. What works for one person may not work for another, so don't be afraid to experiment and discover what makes you feel your best.

Embrace the Healing Power of Music

Music is a gift that we can use daily to improve our mental and physical well-being. Whether you're looking to reduce stress, boost productivity, or simply express yourself, music provides an accessible and effective way to enhance your life. By incorporating music into your daily routine, you can experience its healing benefits firsthand and unlock a deeper connection to yourself and the world around you.

So the next time you feel overwhelmed, anxious, or stuck, turn on some music. Let it carry you through the tough moments and remind you of the joy, creativity, and healing power that exists within you.

CONFLICT RESOLUTION TECHNIQUES FOR A MORE PEACEFUL LIFE

Conflicts can have far-reaching effects if not handled properly. It can occur in various contexts, and understanding that context is crucial to conflict resolution. For instance, a conflict in a marriage often involves children, extended families, and the relational networks of the two partners. If the conflict is not solved, society becomes involved through legal processes that can lead to divorce. The ripples of divorce have far-reaching and somewhat unpredictable consequences.

People generally do not like conflict as it is often "messy" and unpleasant. It can cause emotional damage and affect a person's wellbeing through unresolved, ongoing resentment and bitterness that may remain.

Conflict can be personal or professional. On the individual level, resolving conflict demands focused and reflective listening with an attitude of respect and acceptance of the other person. It also requires affirming and asserting oneself correctly and at the proper time. On the professional level, organizational conflict resolution involves confident, non-defensive leadership and commensurate willingness to envisage win-win solutions (the art of compromise). It can even lead to structural, organizational changes, such as adopting well-conceived and clearly stated policies and procedures (e.g., grievance procedures) and orderly methods by which change is introduced.

It's important to remember that conflict is a natural part of life that can't be avoided entirely. However, it's also important to understand that conflict can be resolved healthily, which benefits everyone involved. Conflicts arise between family members over money or inheritance issues or between coworkers over differences in opinion or work styles. There can be different strategies for resolving conflicts.

Five Strategies to resolve conflict

1. Active Listening

Active listening entails paying great attention to the other person's words without cutting them off or passing judgment. This can help both parties feel heard and understood, which can be an essential first step toward resolving the conflict.

2. Compromise

Compromise involves finding a middle ground where both parties can get some of what they want without giving up everything they're asking for. This can be especially useful when multiple parties are involved in the conflict.

3. Negotiation

Negotiation involves working together to find a solution that works for everyone involved. This might include brainstorming different ideas until everyone agrees on a solution that meets everyone's needs.

4. Mediation

During mediation, a third party who is impartial and who can help facilitate communication between the parties to the conflict is brought in. This can be especially useful when strong emotions are involved or when communication has broken down between the parties.

5. Arbitration

Using both parties' evidence, a neutral third party will arbitrate the dispute and choose how to resolve it. This can be useful when both parties are unable to settle their differences on their own.

It's crucial to keep in mind that there are no dispute resolution strategies that work for everyone.

Instead, it's critical to approach every circumstance with an open mind.

We should be willing to listen and collaborate with others to find a solution that benefits everyone.

SECTION 4
MASTERING WEALTH MANAGEMENT

BECOMING A GOOD MONEY MANAGER

In today's fast-paced world, many of us make money but not necessarily the kind we want or feel we deserve. Often, the issue isn't the amount we make but how we manage what we have. Becoming a good money manager isn't as daunting as it might seem. It starts with making intentional decisions about your finances, evaluating your needs and goals, and exercising self-control when it comes to spending.

Here's a comprehensive guide to help you manage your money and achieve long-term success.

Step 1: Understand Your Needs, Wants, and Goals

To manage your money effectively, you must first assess your financial priorities. Start by listing your **needs** (essential expenses like housing, food, and utilities), your **wants** (non-essential items that improve your quality of life, such as dining out or entertainment), and your **goals** (long-term aspirations like buying a home, saving for a child's education, or retirement).

Once you've identified these categories, prioritize them. For example:

- **Needs**: Rent or loan payments, groceries, insurance.
- **Wants**: Vacation, upgrading your phone, new clothes.
- **Goals**: Saving for a down payment, paying off student loans, or building an emergency fund.

By making this distinction, you'll know where your money should go and where you might need to cut back.

Step 2: Create a Realistic Budget

A budget is the foundation of good money management. Without one, you're likely to overspend, accumulate debt, and struggle to save for the future.

Start by reviewing your income and expenses. Then, allocate your money based on your priorities. For example, if you bring in $3,000 per month, break it down like this:

- **50% for Needs**: $1,500 on rent, groceries, and bills.
- **30% for Wants**: $900 for dining out, subscriptions, etc.
- **20% for Savings and Goals**: $600 towards savings, investments, or debt repayment.

Plenty of apps can help track your spending and ensure you stay on track.

Step 3: Practice Smart Spending

Before making any purchase, ask yourself if it aligns with your goals. For instance, when considering a significant expense like a second vehicle, remember that it's not just the upfront cost—the maintenance, insurance, and interest can make it a substantial financial burden. Do you really need it, or can you make do with one car and save those funds for something more pressing?

Additionally, before you buy anything, take a few minutes to compare prices online. Many retailers offer discounts on the same items you find in stores. Even small savings on everyday items can add up over time.

If you're buying a new laptop, you might find it for $1,000 at a local store, but after checking online, you may find the same model for $850 on an e-commerce platform. That's an instant $150 saved by simply doing some research.

Step 4: Avoid Impulse Purchases

One of the biggest challenges to good money management is the tendency to make impulsive decisions. Whether it's upgrading your phone before you need to or buying the latest gadget, impulsive spending can quickly derail your financial goals.

A simple strategy is to implement a 48-hour rule. If you see something you want but don't necessarily need, wait 48 hours before buying it. Often, after the waiting period, the impulse fades, and you can make a more rational decision.

Step 5: Make Your Money Work for You

Learning to invest is one of the most essential steps in becoming a good money manager. Leaving all your money in a standard savings account earns very little interest, so it's crucial to explore options like:

- **High-Yield Savings Accounts**: These offer better interest rates than traditional accounts.
- **Stock Market Investments**: While risky, they often provide higher returns over the long term. You can invest in individual stocks or low-cost index funds that track market performance.
- **Real Estate**: Purchasing property can be a great way to build wealth if you can afford it.

Warren Buffett is a prime example of someone who's mastered the art of making money work for him. He didn't accumulate fortune by sitting on cash but by making strategic investments in businesses he believed in.

Step 6: Reduce Debt and Build an Emergency Fund

Debt can be crippling, mainly when it accumulates from using credit cards for things you can't afford. Make a conscious effort to reduce your debt, first with the highest interest debts.

At the same time, an emergency fund should be built. Aim to have three to six months' worth of living expenses saved in case of unexpected situations like job loss or medical emergencies. This safety net will protect you from relying on credit cards or loans when life throws surprises your way.

Consider Sarah, a single mother who diligently put aside $200 each month into an emergency fund. After a year, she had $2,400 saved. When her car broke down and needed $1,500 in repairs, she didn't have to use a credit card or take out a loan. Instead, she tapped into her emergency fund, saving herself from additional debt.

Step 7: Plan for the Future

Good money management also means thinking long-term. It's about managing your current finances and planning for retirement and unexpected life events.

Start contributing to a retirement account. Even small, regular contributions will grow over time, thanks to the power of compound interest. Many employers offer matching contributions, essentially free money, so take advantage of this if available.

Learning from Mistakes

Managing money isn't something most people are born knowing how to do. It's a skill that can be developed with time and discipline. You might make mistakes along the way, but the key is to learn from them and adjust your strategies.

For most of us, wealth doesn't come from a windfall but from consistent, careful planning and management. By practicing self-control, setting goals, and making informed decisions, you can build a secure financial future for yourself and your family.

Remember, it's not about how much money you make but how you manage what you have.

SECTION 5
THE PATH TO SPIRITUAL FULFILMENT

WHY YOU SHOULD NEVER LOSE FAITH IN GOD

It's our weakness and privilege to be created with so many needs. We frequently rush to find what our bodies and souls require because we are beings with needs.

It's both our weakness and our strength to want what we desire. Our minds seem to naturally seek delights even when we should be wise enough to resist unfettered desires.

Because our God is so good, he wants to give us everything we need— spiritually, physically, and emotionally. The Bible shows us how he does it: by providing everything we need through Jesus Christ. Many things happen in our lives that we don't understand or find hard to accept at first.

But they soon make sense when we look at them through the Bible. God can make sense of things that seem out of place or difficult to explain. And the Bible helps us see how they really fit into the plan of God for our lives, which is good and perfect. Through Christ, his love is shown in all its fullness so that we may have the hope of eternal life.

Providence refers to the way God takes care of us. It's an old (Greek) word that literally means "arranging things". God always arranges things for our good.

It doesn't have to be something dramatic like a huge windfall or rescue out of prison.

It can be as simple as a phone call from a relative or whenever you enjoy some nice weather after being stuck in the rain for a few days.

Jesus said that He came so that we might have life and have it more abundantly. A relationship with Jesus will provide us more than food, shelter, or clothes. It will give us everything essential to our happiness and satisfaction.

The Bible says:

For God so loved the world that he gave his one and only Son, that whoever believes in him shall not perish but have eternal life.

-John 3:16 (NIV)

This points to how good being part of God's family is. God took care of the needs of His children when they lived down here on earth, and He'll do it again when we are a part of His family living with Him someday in heaven.

The Bible says:

25 "Therefore I tell you, do not worry about your life, what you will eat or drink; or about your body, what you will wear. Is not life more than food, and the body more than clothes? 26 Look at the birds of the air; they do not sow or reap or store away in barns, and yet your heavenly Father feeds them. Are you not much more valuable than

they? 27 Can any one of you by worrying add a single hour to your life? 28 "And why do you worry about clothes? See how the flowers of the field grow. They do not labor or spin. 29 Yet I tell you that not even Solomon in all his splendor was dressed like one of these. 30 If that is how God clothes the grass of the field, which is here today and tomorrow is thrown into the fire, will he not much more clothe you — you of little faith? 31 So do not worry, saying, 'What shall we eat?' or 'What shall we drink?' or 'What shall we wear?' 32 For the pagans run after all these things, and your heavenly Father knows that you about tomorrow, for tomorrow will worry about itself. Each day has enough trouble of its own. need them. 33 But seek first his kingdom and his righteousness, and all these things will be given to you as well. 34 Therefore do not worry about tomorrow, for tomorrow will worry about itself. Each day has enough trouble of its own.

-Matthew 6:25 - 34 (NIV)

We should not worry about the things of this world, because our life is more than those things.

Worry accomplishes nothing. It does not add to the quality of life or help us to accomplish anything.

Jesus didn't just tell the disciples to stop worrying; He told them to replace their worries with a concern for the kingdom of God. Only through a change in habits or passions can one give up one thing for another.

Jesus Christ reminds us of the importance of living in the present. It is not wrong to remember the past or plan for the future, yet it is easy to become too focused on the past or the future and ignore the day's troubles.

Jesus reminds us that living for the present day is more important than remembering the past or planning for the future. Living for the present day means being aware of your surroundings and engaging with them; it also means not ignoring your problems and choosing to focus on them.

Jesus is enough. As you draw near Him, you'll discover how much He satisfies. Not only does He satisfy you, but He gives you a vision for the future that is so good.

WHY JOHN THE BAPTIST IS IMPORTANT TO THE CHRISTMAS STORY

In the Christmas story, we see the importance of John the Baptist in preparing the way for Jesus Christ.

The Bible tells us that God had sent John to prepare people for Jesus Christ's coming.

And he will go on before the Lord, in the spirit and power of Elijah, to turn the hearts of the parents to their children and the disobedient to the wisdom of the righteous — to make ready a people prepared for the Lord.

-Luke 1:17 (NIV)

This means that John was an important part of God's plan for mankind. He came to tell people about their sins and how they needed to be saved from them. He also told them about Jesus Christ, who would come after him and save them from their sins.

John lived at an important time in history when God was preparing to send His Son into this world to save us from our sins.

as it is written in Isaiah the prophet:
"I will send my messenger ahead of you,
who will prepare your way"
-Mark 1:2 (NIV)

He was also a man who had been prepared and chosen by God. The importance of John the Baptist in the Christmas story is that he was one of the prophets who foretold the coming of the Messiah. John the Baptist was a prophet of God who came to prepare the way for Jesus. John the Baptist was the one who baptized Jesus in the Jordan River, and hence the Old Testament prophecy was fulfilled. The baptism of Jesus has been described in all four gospels.

John the Baptist is one of the most important characters in the Christmas story, and many people are missing it.

Truly I tell you, among those born of women there has not risen anyone greater than John the Baptist; yet whoever is least in the kingdom of heaven is greater than he.
-Matthew 11: 11 (NIV)

John was a prophet who announced Jesus as the Messiah and confirmed that Jesus was, indeed, the Lamb of God.

John replies that he is not when the religious leaders ask him if he is the Prophet, Elijah, or Christ. He actually responds with the humility of "a voice wailing in the desert."

"a voice of one calling in the wilderness,
'Prepare the way for the Lord,
make straight paths for him. "
-Mark 1:3 (NIV)

John's message was not one of self-aggrandizement or self-promotion; it was a call for repentance from sin and a return to God's grace. For this reason, many people have viewed him as a precursor to Jesus Christ and his message as an important part of Christian history.

The Christmas story has been told countless times over the past 2,000 years. The story of Jesus bringing light into darkness has been told by countless artists, poets, and musicians throughout time who have interpreted it in their own way.

But what does this story mean for us today?

This is a key moment in the Christmas story because it shows us that our identity does not come from being a product of our environment but from God's calling on our lives. It also shows us that we don't need to be perfect to be called by God. We can still be forgiven and accepted by God even if we mess up sometimes or even all the time.

The religious leaders sought a Messiah who would bring them glory and honor. They wanted a Saviour who would be born in their own time and place. But Jesus came from afar; he was not one of them. He came with a message of peace and love for everyone, regardless of race or religion.

HOW TO OVERCOME SPIRITUAL FATIGUE AND REKINDLE YOUR PASSION FOR GOD

According to the Word of God, we are commanded to be in the world but not of the world. Yet, living among the ungodly can affect our spiritual health and vitality. We can relate to Moses, who faced constant opposition and rebellion from the people he was leading. His frustration and exhaustion led him to act in anger and disobedience.

How do we recognize the signs of spiritual fatigue in ourselves? How do we prevent it from affecting our relationship with God and others?

The apostle Paul addressed this issue in his letters to the churches in Galatia and Thessalonica. He urged them not to lose heart in doing good, even when they faced persecution or false teaching.

Let us not become weary in doing good, for at the proper time we will reap a harvest if we do not give up.
-Galatians 6:9 (NIV)

However, he did not give specific guidance on how to overcome spiritual fatigue. Spiritual fatigue may manifest itself in various forms. Sometimes, it is evident in our actions and reactions, as it was for Moses. We may become irritable, impatient, or resentful. We may lash out at others or disobey God's commands. Other times, spiritual fatigue is more subtle and hidden. It may show up as complacency or indifference. We may lose our passion and zeal for God and His work. We may neglect our spiritual disciplines or compromise our standards. This was the case for the church in Ephesus, who had abandoned their first love.

Spiritual fatigue is a state of weariness and exhaustion that afflicts the soul and hinders its communion with God. It can have detrimental effects on your personal relationships, your physical health, and your mental well-being. It may also increase your susceptibility to the devil's traps and temptations.

How to Overcome Spiritual Fatigue

The good news is that spiritual fatigue is not a hopeless condition. You can overcome it by turning to God and seeking His grace and guidance.

Following are some achievable steps you can take to address spiritual fatigue:

1.Prayer: Prayer is the most essential and effective means of overcoming spiritual fatigue. It helps you converse with God, pour out your heart and needs before Him, and listen to His voice. Prayer also enables you to conform your will to God's will and receive His peace and joy. You can pray at any time, place, or manner that suits you. You can also use the Psalms as a model for prayer, as they reflect various emotions and situations you may experience.

The Lord is my shepherd, I lack nothing. He makes me lie down in green pastures, he leads me beside quiet waters.

-Psalm 23:1-2 (NIV)

2. Read the Bible: The Bible is the word of God that feeds your soul and transforms your mind. It helps you learn more about God's nature, promises, commands, and purposes for you. It also helps you discover your identity and calling in Christ. Reading the Bible daily can help you grow in faith, wisdom, and understanding. You can also use a Bible reading plan, a devotional book, or a commentary to help you study the Bible more thoroughly.

Jesus answered, "It is written: 'Man shall not live on bread alone, but on every word that comes from the mouth of God.'

-Matthew 4:4 (NIV)

3. Worship: The act of admiring and praising God for who He is and what He has accomplished is known as worship. Worship helps you focus on God's majesty and mercy rather than your troubles and anxieties. Worship also helps you express your thankfulness and love to God and receive His presence and power. You can worship God through singing, music, dancing, art, writing, or any other creative way that honors Him.

I will praise you as long as I live, and in your name I will lift up my hands.
-Psalm 63:4 (NIV)

4. Fellowship: Fellowship is the act of sharing life with other believers who support you, encourage you, challenge you, and pray for you. Fellowship helps you realize that you are not alone in your spiritual journey but part of a larger faith community. Fellowship enables you to experience the love and unity that God desires for His people. You can fellowship with other believers through attending church services, joining a small group, participating in a ministry, or engaging in social activities.

Not giving up meeting together, as some are in the habit of doing, but encouraging one another — and all the more as you see the Day approaching.
-Hebrews 10:25 (NIV)

5. Serve: Serving is the act of offering your time, talents, and resources to assist others in need and further God's kingdom. Serving helps you emulate the example of Christ, who came not to be served but to serve and to give His life as a ransom for many. Serving also helps you discover your gifts and passions and experience joy and fulfillment in being a faithful steward. You can serve God by volunteering at your church or a local charity, mentoring a younger believer, sharing the gospel with someone, or giving generously to a cause.

For even the Son of Man did not come to be served, but to serve, and to give his life as a ransom for many.
-Mark 10:45 (NIV)

6. Rest: Rest helps you restore your strength and energy and renew your spirit and perspective. Rest also helps you obey God's design and rhythm for your life, as He sanctified the Sabbath for your benefit.

Remember the Sabbath day by keeping it holy. Six days you shall labor and do all your work, but the seventh day is a sabbath to the Lord your God. On it you shall not do any work, neither you, nor your son or daughter, nor your male or female servant, nor your animals, nor any foreigner residing in your towns. For in six days the Lord made the heavens and the earth, the sea, and all that is in them, but he rested on the seventh day. Therefore the Lord blessed the Sabbath day and made it holy.
-Exodus 20:8-11 (NIV)

You can rest by observing a day of rest, sleeping well, relaxing your body and mind, or delighting in God's creation.

If you feel weary, discouraged, exhausted, or burned out, spend some time reflecting on your spiritual high points.

Remember how you felt as you turned to God in repentance and faith. Remember the joy and peace that filled your heart as you received His forgiveness and grace. Remember the love and power that He poured out on you through His Spirit. Remember the gifts and talents that He bestowed on you for His glory. Remember the trials and victories that He brought you through by His strength.

Remember the promises and hopes that He gave you through His word.

And remember what He has in store for you. Remember that He is preparing a place for you in His Father's house. Remember that He is coming back for you to take you to Himself. Remember that He will wipe away every tear from your eyes and make everything new.

Remember that He will reward you for your faithfulness and crown you with glory and honor. Remember that He will welcome you into His eternal kingdom and say to you, "Well done, good and faithful servant!"

Remember these things, and let them renew your mind, restore your soul, and rekindle your passion for God.

BREAK-UPS CAN MAKE OR BREAK YOU. THE CHOICE IS YOURS.

Have you ever wondered why people who have gone through a bad break-up behave differently? I have seen the change in the personality of several people who have been betrayed by their partners. They may appear hard or sometimes rude if you ever get a chance to talk with them.

The Bible assures us that

The Lord is close to the brokenhearted and saves those who are crushed in spirit.

-Psalm 34:18 (NIV)

David taught this to the men at the cave at Adullam and they heard it attentively. These men were in debt. They were also distressed; some might be discontent in their lives. They were people with broken hearts.

People with broken hearts may think that God is far away from them, but it's the opposite. God is nearer to them.

We should acknowledge that not every relationship ends up in marriage.

Most of the time, believers tend to act in a worldly way during the breakup. Ending the relationship should be done in a way that is God honoring.

When the relationship is over, it becomes tempting to ponder over the same things repeatedly in our minds and eventually harbor bitterness towards the other person, which is wrong.

Our identity is in Christ; we should not define ourselves by our dating or romantic relationship; even during the break-up, the broken state of our relationship should not define us.

Bear with each other and forgive one another if any of you has a grievance against someone. Forgive as the Lord forgave you.

-Colossians 3:13 (NIV)

We should learn from what Paul says in the verse above. Forgive as the Lord forgave you. You need to forgive your ex-boyfriend or girlfriend as well, especially if your heart was broken.

Your relationship with the other person may not look the same the way it did before you dated. You may need to distance yourself from the person you broke up with by setting essential boundaries so that you can protect your heart. Distancing yourself from the other person emotionally takes time, and that's normal.

God sometimes may end your relationship with the other person because it is not good for your soul.

If the person you dated or were in a relationship with was the highest priority in your life, then it was not good for you. You would have given your partner the first place in your life, but it should be God first.

God might have used your past relationship to refine you so that you draw closer to Him through the past hardships.

We should not put our hope in the person we are dating; instead, we put our trust and hope in God, who never fails and never slumbers.

HAS CHRISTMAS BECOME MORE OF A CAPITALIST SHOW THAN A FESTIVAL?

Whenever I hear of Christmas, I think of the birth of Jesus Christ who was born in a manger, because there was no room for Joseph and Mary in the local inn at Bethlehem. His way of living renounced the procurement of wealth and worldly goods. Jesus warned about the deadly dangers of materialism in his message.

Two thousand years later, if I observe the Christmas celebration in our modern capitalist society, I see a fat, white chubby figure whose white beard is resting on his plump red belly, the one who is called—Santa Claus. Santa is easily recognizable because his image is splashed everywhere, apparently not as a symbol or god to worship but as a decorative marketing tool. He is everywhere, omnipresent, omniscient, compelling people to buy overpriced gifts and load their shopping carts.

He is not that 4th century Saint Nicholas, a Greek-Christian bishop known for distributing gifts and advocating for the poor. The Santa you see today in malls, marketing complexes, and pretty much all around is a creation, promotion and marketing of the Coca-Cola Company. In 1931, the company started placing Coca-Cola ads in popular magazines. Archie Lee, the D'Arcy Advertising Agency executive, working with The Coca-Cola Company, wanted the campaign to portray a realistic Santa, who could be symbolic too. So Coca-Cola commissioned Haddon Sundblom, a Michigan-born illustrator, to develop advertising images using Santa Claus, that showed Santa in the true sense, not someone dressed up as Santa.

Between 1931 and 1964, Coca-Cola advertisements showed Santa Claus delivering toys, pausing to read a letter and enjoying a Coke, visiting children in their homes who stayed up all night to greet him, and sometimes even raiding refrigerators. Do we really want to keep celebrating Christmas in India's Amazon-fuelled consumeristic attitude under the profile of a Coca-Cola-inspired Santa Claus? Christmas is not just a time to exchange gifts, hang stockings, send greetings, have dinners or shout "Merry Christmas". It is, in fact, the time to celebrate the birth of the Messiah who prioritized the poor and the powerless— the shepherds. Being concerned for the poor and the powerless, by not honoring the God of capitalism is the true spirit of Christmas.

India is no stranger to income inequality, the gap, in fact, is widening further. According to the report titled 'Reward Work, Not Wealth[1]' published by OXFAM, India's top 1%

---

[1] Reward work, not wealth | Oxfam International. (2022, May 25). Oxfam International.
https://www.oxfam.org/en/research/reward-work-not-wealth

of the population now holds 73% of the wealth while 67 crore citizens, comprising the country's poorest half, saw their wealth rise by just 1%. Adivasis, Dalits, daily wage workers, marginal farmers, and a large number of Muslims are the victims of multiple inequalities. They are poor economically and face various levels of social discrimination. Indian Exclusion Report (IXR) 2016[2], released by the Centre for Equity Studies (CES) claims that Dalits, Adivasis, and Muslims continue to be the worst-hit communities in terms of exclusion from access to public goods.

Celebrating the birth of Jesus Christ doesn't necessarily require a secret visit from Santa. There's simply no need for Santa to be a part of any of your choices—your internet clicks, your decorations, your cooking at home, your shopping habits, your time with your family.

---

[2] Correspondent, S. (2017, May 11). Dalits, Adivasis, Muslims worst off, says Indian
Exclusion Report. The Hindu.
https://www.thehindu.com/news/national/dalits-adivasismuslims-worst-off-says-indian-exclusion-report/article18427801.ece

SECTION 6
ADDRESSING EVERYDAY CONCERNS

BREAKING BARRIERS AND BUILDING NEW CEILINGS: REFLECTIONS ON GENDER ROLES & SOCIETAL NORMS

Binary gender identity has been the basis for social construct in society since time immemorial, defining gender roles and expectations from both sexes in society, such as men are primarily expected to earn and provide for the family and women are expected to bear children and run the household. However, one's gender assigned at birth does not essentially restrict their role in society, and several examples from modern history can be picked when the gender role reversals have not only been acknowledged but appreciated. One such particular example is women taking a leadership role in politics. Traits such as compassion, aggression, empathy, kindness, and vengeance can be found in any person, irrespective of their sex or gender identity, or even sexual orientation. These characters cannot be confined within the scope of masculinity or femininity. Besides gender identity, the sexual orientation of a person can also differ and there hasn't been a time better than now in the history of modern society when diverse gender expression and orientations have been acknowledged.

Liberalization of the last few decades has led our society to the sexual revolution in more ways than we can understand without doing an indepth study. Liberalization has given us great outcomes such as tolerance of diversity, inclusive society, freedom of expression, and many others at the same time, like any other phenomenon. Still, this revolution has given some unintended outcomes that cannot be categorized positively. Possibly, one of the most tricky and problematic phenomena in this aspect for me as an individual is that, on the one hand, we are more modern than ever that we are ready to land on Mars, whereas, on the other, we cannot let go of the traditional practices no matter how irrelevant they may be today.

Women's autonomy, rights, and agency are not alien to this. In the society where I live, I have seen that women are often expected to act in a certain way, conforming to the norms of the society set thousands of years ago. This has been normalized to the extent that we even teach girls and women to sit in certain ways, eat less, talk less, smile but not laugh loudly, act reserved, be covert, not speak out their minds, have patience, not step out of homes, etc., the list is quite endless. Whereas we control women and girls from the very early stages of their life, we also do certain things beyond my comprehension — for example, objectifying women and setting standards of their body and beauty. If we look at the world of advertising, a new type of woman has been created for the consumption of the desires of society.

To a great extent, our society is conditioned to view women as sexual objects, which have led to women being objectified in every sphere of their life, be it the workplace or home, or on the road.

Just because a woman is working late, staying alone, is friendly with the opposite sex, sexually active, drinks or smokes, she should not be a target to be judged, mistreated, or raped. She is not just someone's wife, partner, girlfriend, daughter, or sister. She is human, and every human being, I believe, is born with the basic right of freedom and dignity.

Sexual objectification and sexism should become a remnant of the past. And with the standards of modern societal development, this should not be only about one gender but about every human being, whether their kind is in the majority or minority, whether they identify as heterosexual or homosexual, whether they follow the gender which was assigned to them at their birth or they have broken themselves free from the expected societal norms and roles attached to their gender.

HIV & COVID-19: WHY NOW IS THE RIGHT TIME TO RE-EVALUATE THE WAY FORWARD

The COVID-19 outbreak reminds us of the initial stage of the HIV epidemic, especially the stigma and discrimination aspect of it. In HIV context, stigma and discrimination ranging from denial of acceptance in the family and community, denial from treatment at hospitals, barring from educational institutes, and termination from workplaces were commonly faced by people living with HIV. Similar to COVID-19 crisis, there was an atmosphere of uncertainty and distress among the general public due to inaccurate and incomplete information.

To fight the COVID-19 epidemic, prompt political commitment and special task force teams were set up, and a large number of volunteers and huge donations were mobilized in a short period but lacked active engagement of civil societies, unlike in the case of HIV.

The lessons learnt from the national HIV programme addressing stigma and discrimination can be applied well in the context of COVID-19.

To generate awareness and spread accurate information, testimonial sharing, especially by celebrities who have recovered from COVID-19, will be very effective in dispelling myths and misconceptions associated with the virus and reinforcing the positive messages.

Learning from HIV response, the pre and post-test counseling to COVID-19 patients will enable them to cope better. Effective engagement of civil societies, faith-based organizations, and affected community members in creating an enabling environment, sensitization of local leaders, and safeguarding the people affected by COVID-19, especially healthcare workers and essential service providers, from being stigmatized and discriminated against, will strengthen the COVID-19 response.

Affected people-led advocacy to district and state authorities to address gaps in healthcare facilities will prove to be highly effective. Setting up a grievance redressal and stigma discrimination response mechanism is imperative to ensure a timely response to any stigma/ discrimination faced by the general population, including healthcare workers and essential service providers.

India has so far done well in taking measures to contain the spread of COVID-19.

The increased number of daily tests, expansion of hospital facilities, policies and guidelines for self-quarantine, and widespread public health awareness messages- all have contributed to minimizing the harmful impact on public health.

The epidemic is not over yet. Some lessons we have learned from the HIV or TB response will be helpful in defeating COVID-19. We have in the past defeated polio, we must remain resilient in our fight against COVID-19.

AN INSIGHT INTO AN INDIAN STATE YOU KNOW TOO LITTLE ABOUT

Mizoram is one of the seven northeastern states of India, bordered by Myanmar (formerly known as Burma) to the east and south, Bangladesh to the west, and by the states of Manipur, Assam, and Tripura to the north.

The Mizos are divided into several tribes – the *Lushais, Pawis, Paithes, Raltes, Pang, Himars, Kukis etc.* Society is based largely around tribal villages. Village life focuses on the chief 's house and the zawlbuk (community house for young, single men). Mizo and English are the official languages. The literacy rate in Mizoram is about 91%, one of the highest in India. More than 80 percent of the population comprises Christians, of which the larger strength is of Protestants, who were converted by missionaries during the 19th century. There are Muslim, Buddhist, and Hindu minorities. The itinerant Chakmas profess an amalgamation of Hinduism, Buddhism, and animism (i.e. the worship of nature deities and other spirits).

While mostly Christians, the hill people have kept alive their rich cultural heritage, colorful customs, and lively traditions. An interesting tradition amongst the Mizos is the code of ethics, which revolves around *tlawmngaihna*, an untranslatable term which means that every Mizo is duty-bound to be hospitable, kind, unselfish, and helpful to the poor and needy.

The most popular dances of Mizoram are *Cheraw* (Bamboo dance), *Khuallam* (dance for visitors or guests), *Chheih Lam* (at the end of a day's work) and *Solakar* or *Sarlamkai* (prevalent among the *Mara* and *Pawl* tribes).

The Mizo Society is basically patriarchal in nature where male dominance is prevalent. The husband, being the head of the family, exercises unfettered and autocratic dominance over his wife and other members of the family. The power and authority of the patriarch over his children is almost unlimited.

As such, in the past, women were not treated as equal to their male counterparts. The status of the Mizo women in the family was so wretched. Women undertook all responsibilities in the family without authority. In spite of all the sacrifices rendered to the family, the wife has still found herself insecure as she may be terminated and divorced by her husband anytime.

Divorce, or separation, on any ground, was a serious matter. If the bride was divorced, she had no claim except on her own properties. If the divorce was, however, due to adultery, she had nothing to claim including her own properties.

With regards to birth, both male and female children were treated with equal joy. Birth of a female child brought as much happiness in the family as that of the male child. Right from her childhood, a girl child made herself available to the parents and assisted them as much as she could. There is one old Mizo saying, *"Crab's meat is not counted as meat, as women's word is not counted as word. Bad wife and bad fence can be changed. But the unthreatened wife and unthreatened grass of the fields are both unbearable".*

As the Mizos follow the patriarchal system, the right to inherit the property was denied to the women and the children belonged to the father, as the descent is traced from the father's side. The Mizo women were also found to perform more work than men, from cleaning the *jhum* (slash and burn cultivation), sowing seeds, cleaning weeds, harvesting, and transporting the harvest from *jhum* to the house. Not only that, she had also undertaken all the household chores.

Mizo women did not have a part to play in performing religious and other sacrificial rites. All these rites were performed by the male members only. A woman could not become a priest called *Bawlpu* or *Sadawt*.

Dowry, or bride price, was also practiced by the Mizo society. The girl was purchased and the price was distributed among the relatives of both paternal and maternal lines. The bride came to the husband's house with *Thuam* (dowry), which consisted of *Thival* (bead with three strings) or *Thifen* (bead with one string) or an amber worth not less than Rs.20/-, or cash not less than Rs.20/-.

However, the advent of Christianity and the expansion of education brought about tremendous changes in the status of the Mizo women. Women are no longer considered inferior to their male counterparts. Women, today, are self-confident and self-reliant. They have contributed to the Mizo society's political, social and economic upliftment. The bride price is still prevalent because they seek to preserve the customs that their grandparents once practiced. Today, women's participation and suggestions are respected by men. Women hold respectable jobs from primary school teachers to officers' rank in government services and universities. They actively participate in several social activities to promote the living standards and better social conditions of the Mizo society in general, particularly women.

Women empowerment has become a global issue, and the question of the Mizo women's political empowerment needs to be considered in the perspective of what is being done and implemented in East Asia and the South-east Asian region. Only democratization and empowerment can provide Mizo women an avenue through which they can continue their long journey towards total emancipation. To be more specific, two political mechanisms may be considered in this regard: increased proportional representation of women in all elected bodies and fixation of a certain quota of offices therein; and the increased political activities by autonomous women's bodies. Then and only then can she be among the policy-making elites who decide on the overall improvement of women's status.

GENDER EQUITY IN STEM EDUCATION: OVERCOMING CHALLENGES AND EMBRACING OPPORTUNITIES IN INDIA

STEM (Science, Technology, Engineering, and Mathematics) education educates students in four distinct fields — science, technology, engineering, and mathematics. STEM education was introduced in 2001 by scientific administrators at the U.S. National Science Foundation (NSF). The growth of STEM education has picked up significantly over the last few years. One of the nations that produces the most scientists and engineers is India.

However, despite the increasing demand and opportunities for STEM careers, there needs to be more participation of girls in STEM education and fields in India.

According to the Annual Survey of Education Report (ASER) 2018, boys outperform girls in mathematics significantly, which has persisted over time in India. The difference in reading scores is negligible, but there is a considerable variation across the states of India.

According to a UNICEF report[3], globally, only 18 percent of girls in tertiary education are pursuing STEM studies, compared to 35 percent of boys.

This gap has profound implications for girls' future academic and career success and the country's economic and social development.

Reasons for the gap

Gender stereotypes, biases, and attitudes that limit girls' choices and opportunities are key factors contributing to the low involvement of females in STEM education and careers. Many girls face social and cultural barriers that discourage them from pursuing STEM subjects and careers. We frequently hear statements like "Science and maths are for boys, and arts and humanities are for girls," indicating the stereotyping endorsed by parents, relatives, neighbors, and even school teachers. Such messages undermine the confidence and interest of girls in STEM subjects and limit their aspirations.

The lack of mentors and female role models in STEM professions is another factor in females' low participation rates. Many girls do not have access to female scientists, engineers, mathematicians, or technologists who can inspire and guide them. They also need to see more representation

---

[3] Mapping gender equality in STEM from school to work. (n.d.). UNICEF Office of Global
Insight & Policy.
https://www.unicef.org/globalinsight/stories/mapping-gender-equalitystem-
school-work

of women in STEM fields in textbooks, media, or curricula. This creates a perception that STEM fields are not suitable or welcoming for girls.

A key reason for the low participation of girls is the socio-economic status and other factors that affect their access to quality education, health care, safety, and mobility. Many girls face challenges such as poverty, child marriage, childbirth, household responsibility, sexual harassment, and other forms of gender-based violence that reduce their time and resources to study and pursue their interests. Many girls also drop out of school or are forced to choose subjects considered more convenient or appropriate for them by their families or society.

Steps taken by the government and other stakeholders

The government and other stakeholders have taken various steps to address these challenges and promote STEM education among girls.

The government has launched many schemes and policies to encourage girls to enroll and excel in STEM education, such as *Beti Bachao Beti Padhao, Kishori Shakti Yojana, Pragati (Scholarship Scheme for Girls)*, etc.

Many NGOs and civil society groups have also been working to raise awareness about the importance of STEM education for girls and provide them with mentoring, guidance, counseling, scholarships, etc. These non-governmental organizations work with schools, communities, parents, teachers, etc., to create a supportive environment for girls to pursue STEM education and careers.

Many role models and influencers have also emerged in recent years, inspiring many girls to follow their dreams in STEM fields. Some examples are Kalpana Chawla (the first Indian woman astronaut), Kiran Mazumdar-Shaw (the founder of Biocon), Indra Nooyi (the former CEO of PepsiCo), Sudha Murty (the chairperson of Infosys Foundation), etc.

Solutions for the gap

To address these challenges and promote STEM education among girls, various steps need to be taken by different stakeholders.

The government should implement policies and programs encouraging girls to enroll and excel in STEM education at all levels. This includes providing scholarships, incentives, infrastructure, equipment, curriculum reform, teacher training, etc. The government should also monitor and evaluate the impact of these policies and programs on gender equality in STEM education.

The schools should provide a supportive environment for girls to pursue STEM subjects and careers. This includes creating gender sensitive classrooms, eliminating gender bias and stereotypes in teaching and learning materials, providing exposure to female role models and mentors in STEM fields, and organizing extracurricular activities that foster interest and engagement in STEM subjects.

Parents and communities should support the choices and aspirations of girls in STEM subjects and careers. This includes challenging gender stereotypes and norms that limit girls' potential, guiding and encouraging girls to pursue their interests and talents, and respecting their autonomy and agency in making decisions about their education and future.

The media and society should raise awareness about the importance and benefits of STEM education for girls and women. This includes showcasing the achievements and contributions of women in STEM fields, highlighting the opportunities and challenges they face, celebrating their diversity and creativity, and challenging the myths and misconceptions about their abilities and roles.

In addition to being a subject of fairness and justice, closing the gender gap in STEM education is an immediate matter of necessity and opportunity. By empowering girls with STEM skills and knowledge, we can unleash their potential to become innovators, leaders, and changemakers who can shape a better future for themselves and others.

NETFLIX'S DELHI CRIME: A REALISTIC PORTRAYAL OF STRONG WOMEN CHARACTERS

Based on case files from the Delhi Police, the first season of Netflix web series – Delhi Crime released on March 22, 2019, as a dramatic recreation of behind the scenes investigation of the ghastly Nirbhaya gang-rape case (in which a 23-year-old para-medical student was gangraped and brutally assaulted by six men in Delhi in December 2012).

This shook the conscience of the citizens of India. The seven-part web series created, written and directed by Indo-Canadian filmmaker Richie Mehta covers a six-day period between December 16 and 21 2012—the horrific incident day to the final arrest day.

Delhi Crime shows how the police officials quickly responded to the incident and nabbed the six culprits in five days. The lead cast of this series are DCP of South District – Vartika Chaturvedi (Shefali Shah), Head of Special Task Force-Bhupinder Singh (Rajesh Tailang), Delhi Police Top officer and Vartika's husband – Vishal Chaturvedi (Denzel Smith), teenage daughter of Vartika – Chandni (Yashaswini Dayama), Commissioner of Police – Kumar Vijay (Adil Hussain), trainee IPS Officer – Neeti Singh (Rasika Dugal), SHO of Vasant Vihar Police Station – Vinod Tewari (Vinod Sharawat), female victim – Deepika (Abhilasha Singh) and Deepika's friend – Akash (Sanjay Bishnnoi).

Vartika leads the investigation team and displays the characteristics of a true leader. She is the mother of a teenage daughter – Chandni who does not want to stay in Delhi as it's 'unsafe' according to her. Vartika's trusted aide, Bhupinder is always found supportive and understands that criminal cases cannot be solved through emotion.

As the series proceeds, Vartika forms a dedicated team of police officers picked up from various police stations in Delhi. The team consists of Vimla Bharadwaj (Jaya Bhattacharya), Sudhir Kumar (Gopal Datt Tiwari), Narayan (Chandan Kumar), Subhash Gupta (Sidharth Bhardwaj), and Jairaj (Anurag Arora), who work tirelessly to nab the offenders.

Neeti Singh is given the responsibility to take care of Deepika and her ailing family (mother, father and a brother) and be available for them. She is also called out to attend the protest duty at India Gate. Neeti, in order to become an independent woman, has moved from Chandigarh to Delhi. She becomes emotionally attached with the victim and their family and is even seen weeping behind closed doors of a washroom seeing the critical condition of the victim, Deepika. Neeti's character showcases the true nature of humanity as she carries out her assigned duty selflessly and even by sacrificing her personal needs.

The other strong woman character, **Vimla** even after knowing the brutality of the crime committed by the sixth culprit- Sonu, who appears to be minor, does not allow her colleagues to book him in this case as an adult. She carried out her duties according to the book as a juvenile affairs officer. Vimla did not let her emotions overpower her priority and her duty towards the law. Vimla is also lectured by Vartika to improve her English and asked to seek the support of DCP's daughter, Chandni.

Chandni finds Delhi unlivable, the only way out according to her is to move out of the country and go to Canada for higher studies. Chandni is found joining the protest against Delhi Police and even shown slapping one of her classmates speaking against the corrupt police officials. Her mother repeatedly assures Chandni that Delhi is becoming safer, but she has her own set of beliefs and instincts.

It is daunting to watch the entire series at one go, as the viewers will be constantly reminded of the horrific incident that happened in 2012 and cannot be washed easily from our collective memories. This is a show worth watching and once you have started you will watch this till the end. The dialogues are often filled with dark humour at times to relieve the intense set of events happening one after another.

When Sudhir Kumar (Gopal Datt Tiwari) is asked by his subordinate, *"How can someone do this to another person?"* (Questioning the intent behind such a horrifying crime) he replies— *"It's simple. It's in economics. The bigger the gap between the rich and poor, the more the crimes. You see, the rich have brought more money into society. But it's not reaching the poor. So they try and take it. The result is more strife in society. It's normal. It's happening all over the world. Add to that the explosion of uneducated youth here. They have no sex education but get free porn online which affects their adolescent brains. They don't know how to interpret it. They objectify women and wish they could have that in their lives. If they don't get it, they take it, with no regard for the consequences. After all, they have nothing to lose."*

The first episode starts with an introduction which states — *"Delhi- India, the Capital City. It has the population of a small country. 11,000 heinous crimes are reported every year. Prevention is nearly impossible with half the police force stuck on traffic duty and VIP protection. The city looks away because it has to. Because it always has. But once something happened, which made it stop. For a moment, the eyes of the entire world turned to Delhi. It was the crime that took the city to the brink."*

This web series celebrates the valour of the Delhi Police and shows the other side of the story as the viewers are compelled to empathize for them. While the entire world was criticizing them, they faithfully carried out the investigation to nab the accused. The grit and determination exhibited by the leading female characters draw a glimpse of hope of a safer and stronger future. Delhi Crime is more to change the general public's perception towards the police machinery and I find it positive. Richie Mehta has done a marvelous job with the help of a dynamic team of actors who have justified their roles and connected with the viewers in every scene.

REVIEW: NETFLIX'S 'HOUSE ARREST' FAILS TO EXPLORE SHADES OF URBAN LONELINESS

'House Arrest' is a movie about a young ex-banker, who has consciously decided to stay inside his spacious and luxurious apartment for nine months, and shut himself up from the outside world. This Netflix Original movie was released on 15 November 2019 and directed by Samit Basu and Shashanka Ghosh.

Karan (Ali Fazal) has found his best friend in JD (Jim Sarbh) who calls him while urinating, taking a massage, gyming and post-sex. Karan and JD have been friends since school. JD sends a journalist friend Saira (Shriya Pilgaonkar), to Karan's house for an interview. Saira is a journalist who has never been shown taking notes, writing on a notepad or even recording the interview in the movie. Maybe the director relied on her utter intelligence, assuming she would remember every bit of the interview.

Karan has a quite chirpy neighbour, Pinky (Barkha Singh) who hands him a pink suitcase with the help of her extremely tall and hefty bodyguard, Rambo. The content of the suitcase seems suspicious. One intriguing thing about Pinky is that to justify her name, she has been shown wearing pink clothes, pink lipstick, pink hairbands, and pink hairstreaks. She is an over-friendly Delhi girl, and her character in the movie is something viewers may remember.

The movie starts with a radio announcement, *"Hello, Delhi! It's eight o'clock on Monday and we're all off to work. The traffic is terrible. But of course, darling, this is NCR's Delhi. If you are stuck in your car making lists of the battles you are fighting this week with your rivals, colleagues, and clients, there must be a little thought in some corner of your mind, wondering why Sunday ended at all. Man, why did I leave the house at all? I could be curled in bed, doing nothing. After all, there's no place like home".*

The above announcement sets the tone for the 104-minutes-long movie. Karan admits that the entire world is looking for ways to get him out of the house and is unsure how long he will be able to carry on like this. In Karan's character, viewers will find some traits of Mirzapur, sadly it fades away suddenly. Karan talks about the concept of zero physical and social contact, rejecting society – Hikikomori.

Saira believes that Karan is not alone but lucky. She thinks that Karan has many friends and family members who care about him and want to see him happy. Confessing her state, she says that if she decides to stay home and cut herself off from society, weeks would pass by and no one would notice.

The entire concept of urban loneliness has not been explored on a serious note in the movie. There are bits and pieces of it spread across the entire movie length, but who has the time to collect those pieces together? The responsibility is on the writer who has written the script. Leaving it in the hands of the viewer has left this movie a bit mundane.

Karan just wants one day where no one would disturb him. Will he be able to accomplish that goal? If you are interested in his destiny, you can go and watch this movie.

The love chemistry between Karan and Saira will, of course, keep you captivated.

ZEE5 'POISON' REVIEW: WHEN LOVE TURNS TO LUST AND REVENGE BECOMES POISONOUS

Zee5 Original "Poison" released on 19 April 21, 2019, is a Crime thriller revolving around the characters- Ranveer (Tanuj Virwani), Vikram (Freddy Daruwala), Antonio Verghese (Arbaaz Khan), Natasha (Riya Sen) and others. The narrative is set around two cities- Mumbai and Goa. The lead character Ranveer, completes his 7-year term in Arthur Jail, Mumbai and moves to Goa after selling his ancestral property at a throwaway price. In Goa, he has to deal with the local don Dominic, who is backed by the drug lord Antonio Verghese but Ranveer has come to Goa with a different purpose.

The 11-episode web series, directed by Jatin Wagle and written by Shiraz Ahmed narrates the intricacies of love turning into lust greed causing the loss of distinction between right and wrong in the conscience of characters leaving the victim with a poison of revenge in their heart.

The narrative of Shiraz Ahmed is filled with various multilayered characters who have their individual hidden agenda and they can go to any extent to fulfil them. Dialogues are quite filmy in this web series. The owner of Cheetos club, Moses describing the character of his boss Dominic Dixon in the second episode, says, *"Saboot ungliyaan unkon pasand nahin, ye dekh rahe ho-pahli baar mein ungli, dusri baar mein haath aur teesri baar mein mut karne wali jagah nahi chhorte, daya itni karte hain ki kisiko jaan se nahin maarte, dayawaan jo thehre humaare boss Dominic Dixon". (Full fingers he doesn't like, (If you make a mistake) see this — In the first time-finger, second time- the hand and the third time he doesn't even spare your genitals, he shows kindness and doesn't kill anyone, kind and merciful is our boss, Dominic Dixon.")*

Vikram, DSP by designation has the ambition of becoming a Police Commissioner. Will he be able to achieve his ambition? Will Vikram manage to save his family? You will have to watch this web series to know the future of Vikram. Vikram stays with his wife, Megha and two sisters- Ashu and Jahnvi. Ranveer's character is confident and very clear about his life goals. Ranveer plans and executes them faithfully with the help of various aides in his journey. There is yet another interesting character, Rani, who is ready to join hands with anybody, whether with the cops or the bad guys. Rani's character is quite sensational, more than that of Natasha.

While watching the web series produced by Altus Media, sometimes my sympathies were with Ranveer and sometimes with Vikram. These two characters' constant change of emotions stayed till the last episode.

ACKNOWLEDGMENTS

It's hard for me to believe I'm writing a book's acknowledgments. As I sit down to pen these words of gratitude, I am acutely aware that no book is genuinely the work of a single individual. It is a collective effort, a journey filled with the support and encouragement of countless souls who believe in the power of words.

First and foremost, I express my most profound appreciation to my family. To my mother and father, you have been my guiding stars, nurturing my love for words and storytelling since my earliest days. Your unwavering support and belief in my creative journey have inspired me. Your sacrifices and encouragement have paved the way for this book to come to life.

To my younger brother, Akash, your friendship and inspiration have been invaluable. Your perspective and insights have enriched these pages more than you can imagine. You've been a pillar of strength, and I'm lucky to have you by my side.

To my beloved wife, Jyoti, you are my muse, confidante, and biggest cheerleader. This book would not be what it is without your love and support.

In the quiet moments of reflection, it becomes evident that every creation, every endeavor, and every journey is infused with a force greater than ourselves. With a humble heart, I express my deepest appreciation to the divine presence that has guided my path.

To God, I offer my heartfelt gratitude for the profound blessings that have made this book possible. Your gift of life is the canvas upon which this story unfolds, and I am acutely aware of the privilege it is to breathe, dream, and create. Your divine inspiration, the spark that ignites the writer's soul, has illuminated my path and fueled the words on these pages. Your grace has carried me through the darkest writer's block and the brightest creative bursts.

It is through the tapestry of experiences, both joyous and challenging that this book has taken shape. I am grateful for the highs that have filled my heart with wonder and the lows that have deepened my understanding. Every moment and encounter has contributed to the stories woven within these pages.

And finally, the opportunity to share these stories with the world is a gift I do not take lightly. I thank God for reaching out to readers, touching lives, and making a connection through the written word. It is a profound honor to be a conduit of storytelling, and I cherish this calling with all my heart.

This book is a testament to the divine guidance that has infused every word, every sentence, and every page. I offer my unending gratitude to God for being the ultimate source of inspiration and strength throughout this journey.

I extend my deepest gratitude to my cherished circle of prayerful souls, and the remarkable men and women dispersed across the world, from the bustling streets of New Delhi to the serene landscapes of New Jersey. Your unwavering prayers, spanning countless months, have been the silent yet powerful force behind the creation of this book. The bountiful harvest of your intercession is eloquently displayed within its pages, and I have faith that many will partake in the feast of inspiration and wisdom, all thanks to the invisible but profound labor of your hearts.

I extend my sincerest thanks to the incredible team at Kalamos Literary Services, who have worked tirelessly to bring this book into the world. Your dedication, professionalism, and belief in my work have made this journey seamless.

I extend my warmest thanks to my readers, who will embark on this literary adventure. Your curiosity, willingness to explore these pages, and engagement with the book mean the world to me. Without you, these words would remain silent on the page. I am praying God uses this book to help shape you into exactly who he wants you to become.

In the vast universe of publishing, it takes a village to birth a book, and I am privileged to have such an extraordinary village surrounding me. This book is a testament to the love, support, and dedication of the people mentioned here and many others who have touched my life in countless ways. Thank you from the bottom of my heart.

With love and gratitude,
Anurag Paul

ABOUT THE AUTHOR

Anurag Paul (he/him) is a seasoned journalist turned podcaster, renowned for his role as the host of the widely acclaimed podcast show "Life Talks with Anurag Paul." With a background rooted in journalism, Anurag has transitioned seamlessly into the realm of podcasting, where he skillfully intertwines his passion for storytelling with his innate curiosity about life's myriad facets.

Currently serving as the Communications Lead at the International Center for Research on Women (ICRW) Asia, Anurag brings over a decade of expertise to his multifaceted role. Adept at managing communication strategies, program advocacy, and social and behavior change initiatives, he has carved a niche for himself as a dynamic and forward-thinking communicator.

Transformative contributions across various sectors have marked Anurag's journey. As a former Program Officer, Communication at John Snow Inc. (JSI), he played a pivotal role in enhancing the Immunisation Technical Support Unit's social media presence in collaboration with India's Ministry of Health and Family Welfare.

At the India HIV/AIDS Alliance (Alliance India), Anurag led the charge in digital communication, revolutionizing internal and external mechanisms to elevate the organization's profile among stakeholders. His innovative approaches to documenting project implementation and community-driven strategies have championed Alliance India's mission, contributing to its outreach efforts and engagement with key populations.

Anurag's illustrious career has seen him leave his mark on Nobel Peace Prize-winning organisation, Doctors Without Borders/Médecins Sans Frontières (MSF), where he contributed to advocacy projects at the South Asia Office. His journey has been punctuated by collaborations with prominent media outlets such as Press Trust of India (PTI) and NewsGram, showcasing his versatile expertise and holistic understanding of media landscapes.

With a profound knack for building partnerships and spearheading projects aimed at amplifying grassroots voices, Anurag has carved a legacy of elevating community narratives. His journey from journalism to podcasting and his transformative contributions to public health communication stand as a testament to his unwavering dedication to empowering and enlightening diverse audiences.

Education: Post Graduate Diploma in English Journalism from Indian Institute of Mass Communication, New Delhi, and Bachelor of Arts (Hons.) degree in English Literature from Delhi University.

Anurag is an International Council for Evangelical Theological Education (ICETE) Fellow.

Connect with the Author

Facebook: @anuragpaulm

Instagram: @anuragpaulm

Twitter: @anuragpaulm

LinkedIn: @anuragpaul

Email: info@lifetalkswithanuragpaul.com

PODCAST: LIFE TALKS WITH ANURAG PAUL

The podcast "Life Talks with Anurag Paul" inspires people to live the best life - where they can focus on their passions, enjoy meaningful relationships, and discover meaning in everything they do.

Scan the QR code to know more-

9 788119 601271